ISLAMIST NETWORKS

MARIAM ABOU ZAHAB
OLIVIER ROY

Islamist Networks

The Afghan–Pakistan Connection

TRANSLATED FROM THE FRENCH BY JOHN KING

Columbia University Press
New York

*in association with the Centre d'Etudes et de
Recherches Internationales, Paris*

Columbia University Press
Publishers since 1893
New York
Copyright © 2004 Mariam Abou Zahab and Olivier Roy
All rights reserved

ISBN 0-231-13364-2

A Cataloging-in-Publication Data record is available
at the Library of Congress

Columbia University Press books are printed on
permanent and durable acid-free paper.

c 10 9 8 7 6 5 4 3

Contents

Glossary

This summary only lists terms relating to religious practice and expressions which are untranslated, or insufficiently explained. No ethnic groups or place names are given, since these are indicated on the maps.

Ahmadis
: Members of a Muslim sect created in 1889 in the Punjab by Mirza Ghulam Ahmad, who regarded himself as a prophet. It contradicted the Islamic belief that Muhammad was the 'seal of prophecy' (i.e. the final prophet).

Barelvis
: Adherents of a traditionalist movement which appeared in the 1880s under the leadership of Ahmed Riza Khan in reaction to the Deobandi movement. In the majority in rural areas, the Barelvis are characterised by the importance they ascribe to the veneration of saints and their especial devotion to the Prophet Muhammad.

Caliphate
: The spiritual and political headship of the Sunni Muslim community.

da'wa
: Preaching, proselytism. Literally the 'call' to accept Islam.

Deobandis
: The adherents of the reformist movement based on the Deobandi *madrasa*, founded in 1867, which expounds the fundamentalist inheritance of Shah Waliullah.

jihad
: Literally, 'struggle' in the way of God. The 'great *jihad*', an internal (personal) moral and spiritual struggle, is distinguished from the 'lesser *jihad*', holy war for the defence or expansion of Islam.

fatwa
: An opinion given by a jurist (a Mufti), usually on a point of law, which it is not obligatory to follow.

fidayin
: The plural of '*fida'i*', a person who sacrifices himself for a cause.

Hadith
: An oral tradition recounting the words and acts of the Prophet.

madrasa
: A religious school, offering theological and juridical instruction.

Muhajirs
: Muslims who migrated from India to Pakistan after the partition of British India in 1947.

mujahidin	Plural of '*mujahid*', warriors in the holy war.
Mushrif	Literally, a commander or one who supervises. A rank within Hizb ul-Tahrir.
purdah	Literally 'curtain', from the Urdu. The system of segregation of women.
Sahaba	The companions of the Prophet Mohammed. Refers particularly to the three first Caliphs Abu Bakr, Umar and Uthman.
salafi	Fundamentalist who preaches a return to the Islam of the contemporaries of the Prophet Muhammad, purged of local customs and cultures (from *salaf*, ancestor).
shabab	Plural of '*shab*'. An Arabic expression which means 'young men'.
shari'a	The corpus of models and obligations contained in the Quran and the Sunna, which make up Muslim law.
Shi'ites	Partisans of Ali, the cousin and son-in-law of the Prophet Muhammad. The Shi'ites, who believe the Caliphate is rightly exercised by Ali and his descendants, represent a little over 10 per cent of the Muslims in the world.
Sikhs	Followers of a religion founded in the sixteenth century by Guru Nanak.
Sunna	Literally 'custom' or 'usage'. The corpus of deeds, acts, words and opinions of the Prophet Muhammad.
Sunnis	Those who follow the Sunna. The doctrinal majority in Islam.
Tabligh	Literally 'announcement'. A missionary movement founded in 1927 by Muhammad Ilyas in northern India with the goal of re-Islamising Muslims. It claims to be non-political.
ulema	The plural of '*alim*'. Scholars and doctors of Muslim law.
umma	The worldwide community of Muslims
Wahhabis	The followers of a religious reformist movement founded in the eighteenth century in the Arabian peninsula by Muhammad Abdul Wahhab. The Wahhabi doctrine, strongly opposed to Shi'ism and Sufism, places its emphasis on the re-affirmation of '*tawhid*', or divine unity.
zakat	Literally 'purification'. The tax legally obligatory on all Muslims under the Shari'a, which represents 2.5 per cent of profits realised during the year.

Abbreviations

GIA	Groupement Islamique Armé
HM	Hizb ul-Mujahidin (Party of the Mujahidin)
HUA	Harakat ul-Ansar (Movement of the Partisans)
HJI	Harakat ul-Jihad ul-Islami (Movement of the Islamic Jihad)
HUM	Harakat ul-Mujahidin (Movement of the Mujahidin)
IMU	Islamic Movement of Uzbekistan
ISI	Inter-Services Intelligence (the Pakistani military intelligence service)
JI	Jamaat-i-Islami (Society of Islam)
JKLF	Jammu and Kashmir Liberation Front
JM	Jaish-i-Muhammad (Army of Muhammad)
JUI	Jami'at-i-Ulema-i-Islam (Society of the Ulema of Islam)
JUP	Jami'at-i-Ulema-i-Pakistan (Society of the Ulema of Pakistan)
LT	Lashkar-i-Taiba (Army of the Pure)
LJ	Lashkar-i-Jhangvi (Army of Jhangvi)
MEI	Mouvement pour l'Etat Islamique (Algeria)
PIR	Tajik Party of the Islamic Resistance
PML	Pakistan Muslim League
PPP	Pakistan People's Party
SMP	Sipah-i-Muhammad-Pakistan (Army of Muhammad-Pakistan)
SSP	Sipah-i-Sahaba-Pakistan (Army of the Companions of the Prophet-Pakistan)
TJP	Tehrik-i-Jafria-Pakistan (Jafria Movement Pakistan [Shi'ite])
TNSM	Tehrik-i-Nifaz-i-Shari'at-i-Muhammadi (Movement for the Application of the Shari'a of Muhammad)
UTO	United Tajik Opposition

Central Asia

Pakistan

1. Introduction

This book is concerned with those movements, based in Pakistan and Central Asia, which advocated the establishment—by means of armed struggle if necessary—either of an Islamic state within the context of an existing state or, at the supranational level, of a Caliphate. The latter, while forming part of transnational networks of solidarity and militancy, like those of Bin Laden, would also operate beyond those geographical regions. Parties which, although they may profess allegiance to Islamic politics, have not so far developed plans for an Islamic state, or which are not connected to supranational movements—as, for example, Rabbani's Jami'at-i-Islami in Afghanistan—will not be examined. On the ideological level the movements studied share two characteristics. They are 'jihadist'—i.e. they argue the necessity of *jihad* to recover 'occupied' Muslim lands, or even to struggle against Muslim regimes regarded as traitorous. And they are 'salafist', in other words they demand a return to a strict Islam, stripped of local customs and cultures.[1] At the same time such movements are often heterogeneous in both their origins and their current positions. Some, such as the Pakistani Jamaat-i-Islami (JI) and the Tadjik Party of the Islamic Renaissance (PIR), whose members are largely intellectuals with a modern education, are related to the ideological, militant and modern framework of the Muslim Brotherhood and Maulana Maududi. Others, by contrast, including the

---

[1] The expression 'salafi jihadist' occurs in the literature of the GIA (Islamic Armed Groups). Cf. Alain Grignard, *La littérature politique du GIA des origines à Djamal Zitouni. Esquisse d'une analyse*, and F. Dassetto, *Facettes de l'islam belge*, Louvain-la-Neuve (Belgium): Academia-Bruylant, 2001.

Pakistani Jami'at-i-Ulema-i-Islam (JUI) and its imitators, are linked to an older religious tradition of conservatism, which has been recently radicalised, especially following the war in Afghanistan. Among these are the Deobandi school, well established among the Pakistani and Afghan *ulema* and in particular exemplified by the Afghan Taliban, and by the Jami'at-i-Ulema-i-Islam and those stemming from it. There are also elements deriving from the Barelvi school, which is traditionally opposed to the Deobandis and professes a more popular and less scholarly Islam.

In fact radicalism and violence bore little relation to the ideological origin of these movements. Former sympathisers of the Muslim Brotherhood, such as the late Ahmed Shah Massoud in Afghanistan or the mullah Abdullah Nouri in Tajikistan, became moderate nationalists, while former conservatives, who were initially to some extent pro-Western, like the head of the Pakistani Jamaat-i-Islami and former ISI generals such as Hamid Gul, today use radically anti-American language and call openly for *jihad*. Muslim Brotherhood circles have tended to lose their influence and even to dissolve into an imprecise 'islamo-nationalism'. This is well exemplified by the Tajik PIR and in the position adopted by Massoud before his death, while radicalism is today practised rather by more traditional movements which have become radicalised in the course of the Afghan war. Avowed religious ideology does not have, or no longer has a direct relationship with activism.

What, therefore, do the movements encountered in the defined geographical region have in common? By definition, all give the Muslim *umma* priority over ethnic or national identities or interests. Even if movements have identified themselves with a precise territorial area, in the way that the Taliban always wished to be recognised as the legitimate government of Afghanistan, or as the Pakistani groups insisted on a Pakistani identity, they have nevertheless refused to be constricted by a regional identification. Mullah Omar literally sacrificed his regime to protect Bin Laden, while the Pakistani radicals fought outside the frontiers of Pakistan. Jamaat al-Tabligh (or Tablighi Jamaat, as it is also known) assembles groups of preachers deliberately composed of different nationalities, and deploys them in countries of which they are sometimes unable even to speak the language.

However, this 'ummist' perspective becomes radical only when expressed in terms of an appeal to *jihad*. Although all jihadist movements which give priority to *jihad* defined as armed struggle against infidels and traitors are salafist, the reverse is not true. Many salafist movements are opposed to armed *jihad*, either tactically or by conviction, and advocate the *da'wa* or "call" to Islam as a preferred form of action. The degree of emphasis on *jihad*, or alternatively on *da'wa*, allows groups engaged in violent action to be distinguished from others. For the jihadists—who include the Jaish-i-Muhammad (JM) (the army of Muhammad), Lashkar-i-Taiba (LT—the Army of the Pure), Harakat ul-Mujahidin (HUM—the Movement of the Mujahidin), and al-Qaida-*jihad* is the way by which Muslims can be united and recalled to the true practice of Islam. The view is that *jihad*, even if it should fail, is instructive and sets an example: thus is because it allows the Muslim masses to be aroused to consciousness, and a distinction to be drawn between true Muslims and the rest. It is evident that in the eyes of Osama bin Laden the attack on the World Trade Centre embodied this practical teaching. On the other hand, "preaching" movements like Jamaat al-Tabligh, based mainly in Pakistan, and Hizb ul-Tahrir (the Party of Liberation) in Uzbekistan place their emphasis on the individual dimension of the faith as the basis for the rebuilding of the *umma*. The view of these movements is that Muslims must first return to the true faith before it becomes possible to issue any call to *jihad*, which is viewed by them principally as a defence mechanism. The Taliban adhere to this tendency. Their best efforts were directed, through the agency of the "Ministry for the Prevention of Evil and the Promotion of Good", towards ensuring that the whole Afghan people would return to the strict practice of Islam. The underlying idea is that when the majority of nominal Muslims have indeed returned to the strict interpretation of Islam, then—whether by the example they set, or because they will in fact be "the best of communities"—they will be able to re-establish the Muslim *umma*.

However, the separation between these two groups is not total. Many members of preaching organisations go over to *jihad*. The most celebrated instance is that of Mullah Omar, but there is also the case of the young American John Walker-Lindh, enrolled as an active combatant by al-Qaida and taken prisoner at the battle of Taloqan in November 2001, who entered by way of the Jamaat al-Tabligh. On the other hand, the failures of *jihad* may restore the persuasiveness of those who argue the primacy of *da'wa*.

The passage to "jihadism" is primarily linked to a strategic and political context, and with the designation of a particular state as the pre-eminent adversary of the Muslims. Today it is pre-eminently the United States that has been designated by the jihadists as the principal enemy.[2] This is true to a lesser extent of Israel and India.

The following pages will enable the reader to appreciate the extent to which the jihadist movements of Central Asia, Afghanistan and Pakistan—after having begun their existence within a purely national framework or with a single purpose, namely the liberation of Afghanistan—have come to form a transnational network with the United States as the special target.

---

[2] In fact events have unfolded exactly as if the jihadists had continued the anti-imperialist, anti-colonial and Third World tradition, which belonged till the 1980s to the lay extreme left or to a nationalist left. The turning point, that is to say the islamisation of anti-imperialism, was the Islamic revolution of 1979 in Iran. The Shi'ite nature of this development meant that it had only a limited impact in Sunni circles.

2. Ex-Soviet Central Asia

In Central Asia three movements are dominant. The two principal ones, the Islamic Movement of Uzbekistan (IMU) and the Tajik Party of the Islamic Renaissance (PIR), are derived from the Party of the Islamic Renaissance (PIR), created in the Soviet Union in September 1990.[1] The ideas of the Soviet PIR were close to those of the Arab Muslim Brotherhood, since its concern was to set up an Islamic state by means of political action, which would not necessarily include the use of arms. The IMU, like the PIR, is linked with movements in territories lying to the south, in Pakistan and Afghanistan. The third movement, Hizb ul-Tahrir, is atypical. Although a branch has recently been established in Pakistan, its origins lie in the West—or, to be exact, in Britain.

The Tajik Party of the Islamic Renaissance (PIR)

As the keystone of the United Tajik Opposition (UTO), the PIR, was one of the principal protagonists of the civil war which fragmented Tajikistan from 1992 to 1997. From May to December 1992 it participated in a coalition government, together with nationalist and democratic elements, before being driven out by the neo-Communists of the Kulabi faction when the PIR took refuge in Afghanistan. The civil war arose more from rivalries between regionally-based factions than from authentically ideological differences. In this conflict the PIR broadly represented the Tajiks from the region of Gharm, and its leadership was entirely from this region.

[1] On the Soviet PIR see Olivier Roy, *La nouvelle Asie centrale ou la fabrication des nations*, Paris: Le Seuil, 1997, p. 234.

The moderate inclination of the Tajik PIR was in evidence at three critical moments. The first of these was in 1991 and 1992 when the movement allied itself with the nationalists and the democrats; the second came in July 1997 when it signed and strictly observed a coalition agreement with the government of President Rahmanov; and the third indication of PIR moderation occurred in October 1997 when an aircraft carrying the PIR leader Mullah Nuri from Teheran to Dushanbe was intercepted by the Taliban. Mullah Omar demanded that Nuri should enter an alliance with the Taliban, but after being freed Nuri in fact supported Rabbani and Massoud against it.

From July 1997 the Tajik PIR was a constituent of a coalition government with the neo-Communists. It renounced armed struggle, although some lower-level commanders in the upper Gharm valley retained their local militias and their contacts with Uzbek Islamic militants. Its recruitment is mostly local, since it remains centred on the Gharm valley. The party is represented in government, in particular through the Ministry for Emergencies held by Mirza Zayiev, allowing it to maintain an armed force which makes possible the inclusion of this small section of the opposition forces within the general framework of the security forces of the Tajik republic.

However, the inclusion of the Tajik PIR in the political process certainly brought about sweeping changes. One consequence was the transformation of a number of its leaders into men of substance with access to state-controlled wealth in the form of privatisations and export licenses, thus re-establishing networks of patronage or local fiefdoms. In this way Qazi Hajji Akbar Touradjanzade, formerly the second-ranking leader of the United Tajik Opposition, bestowed on himself the ownership of the cotton-processing factory at Kafirnehan. The integration of the Tajik PIR into the political structure also entailed the depoliticisation of the low-ranking local commanders, who had been anxious to use their power to control sources of revenue, including the passage of drugs, and also the transit of Uzbek Islamic militants, who paid to be allowed to operate in

Kyrgyzstan. A consequence was that Islamic values, which were in theory strengthened in the regions held by the former United Tajik Opposition, were in reality neglected: for example, as much alcohol was found in these areas as elsewhere. However, the Party of the Islamic Renaissance, as the only real alternative party other than the Communist Party, began surprisingly to attract new supporters in areas such as, bizarrely, the Ismaili region of High Badakhshan, where it had no prior influence. At the same time a new generation of militants appeared who were younger and less ideological, and sought a genuinely political party that would be able to participate at a national level, and not be solely a manifestation of the regionalism of the Gharmi-valley. A representative of this generation was the new PIR official for external affairs, Muhidin Kabiri (also known as Kabirov).

The Islamic Movement of Uzbekistan (IMU)

Renamed the Islamic Movement of Turkestan in the spring of 2001, the IMU was at that point based in Afghanistan, where it was protected by the Taliban. Banned by the Uzbek government, it had opted for armed struggle and regularly launched military operations at Uzbekistan across Tajik and Kyrgyz territory. Its political chief is Tahir Yuldashev, and until October 2001 its military leader was Juma Namangani. Its militant base was concentrated mainly in the Fergana valley. The IMU was in practice a federation of all the activist Islamic groups in Fergana which had sprung up after 1989. Former militants from the Party of the Islamic Renaissance in Uzbekistan are certainly found in its ranks, but none of its senior leaders has emerged from this movement. The leadership of the Party of the Islamic Renaissance has in fact largely disappeared because of its suppression; Abdullah Utaev, was arrested in 1992, and Sheikh Abdul Vali, the imam of the Jamia mosque of Andijan, in 1995.

The two senior figures in the IMU do not themselves appear to have come out of the PIR. Tahir Yuldashev, who was born on 2 October 1968 in Fergana, directed the Adalat movement, whose armed branch was the Army of Islam (Islam Lashkari), which held the town of Namangan for several weeks in the spring of 1992. By his own account Juma Namangani, born on 12 June 1969, had been a Soviet soldier who served in Afghanistan and returned home having accepted the ideas of the *mujahidin*. Both joined the United Tajik Opposition at the time of its flight into Afghanistan in 1992. In 1996 Namangani spent a substantial period in Saudi Arabia, then in May of that year he set up his military headquarters at Kunduz, where he attracted the allegiance of the Afghan Taliban when they definitively captured the region in the summer of 1998. Subsequently the fusion between the IMU, the Taliban and al-Qaida accelerated. The IMU took the opposite direction from that of the Tajik Party of the Islamic Renaissance: instead of becoming a national party, it internationalised itself and embarked on armed conflict. It mounted two military operations aimed at Uzbekistan in August 1999 and August 2000, across Kyrgyzstan, perhaps with the objective of taking control of the mountainous Uzbek enclave of Sukh in side Kyrgyz territory, which was also populated by Tajiks. A number of Japanese geologists were taken hostage, and the subsequent negotiations were undertaken in Islamabad, a clear indication of the IMU's international connections. In 2001 no attack was carried out, since from June onwards the IMU's forces were for the first time directly in action against Massoud, and defended Kunduz when the American armed forces attacked in October 2001. Namangani was killed in the bombing the following month.

This internationalist tendency became particularly explicit when it was announced that the name of the Islamic Movement of Uzbekistan was to be changed to the Islamic Movement of Turkestan.[2] This decision was connected with three objectives: to "de-Uzbekise" the IMU in the context of the extension of

---

[2] The change was denied by Zubayr ibn Abdulrahim, head of the Supreme Religious Council, in an interview in 2 June 2001 on RFE.

its activities into Tajikistan and Kyrgyzstan; to integrate it into the wider perspective of the *jihad* being waged by al-Qaida—which, as will be seen, rejects all identification with any national framework; and to undermine Hizb ul-Tahrir, whose explicit aim continued to be the establishment of a Caliphate, first of all in Central Asia and then worldwide.

Hizb ul-Tahrir (Party of Liberation)

A new arrival in 1996, Hizb ul-Tahrir was derived from the party of the same name based in London, which itself was the most recent incarnation of a party originally set up as a Palestinian Islamic movement in 1953 which had retreated to London in the 1980s. Although it was officially non-violent, its ideas were very radical, especially since it advocated the immediate re-establishment of the Caliphate. Both clandestine and unknown, it nevertheless enjoyed considerable popularity among the educated but rootless youth of Uzbekistan, with some penetration in the south of Kyrgyzstan and the north of Tajikistan. In contrast to the two parties previously discussed, it had no specific regional base, although it appeared to recruit mainly among ethnic Uzbeks. However from the beginning of 2001 some penetration among the Tajiks and ethnic Kyrgyyz was observed, when the first arrests of its members took place in Dushanbe. The movement did not seem to have links with the Taliban.

Documents published by Hizb ul-Tahrir in Central Asia appear to be word-for-word translations of documents published in Arabic in the Middle East, sometimes even containing Arabic expressions such as *shabab*, designating young militants.[3] The movement was organised in secrecy in cells of five individuals, with each cell kept separate under the leadership of a

---

[3] The web site is *http://www.hizb-ul-tahrir.org*. Translation of Hizb ul-Tahrir's texts has been undertaken by the journal *Cyber Karawan*, 1/8 May 1999, SAIS, Johns Hopkins School, Washington, DC.

mushrif, who was the only person to know the members of other cells. Hizb ul-Tahrir divided the world into provinces, since it rejected the framework of nation-state. It defined itself as "a political party of which the ideology is Islam".

Hizb ul-Tahrir employs extremely radical language. In its view, there can be nothing in common between Western values and those of the Islamic world, and no participation in Western political systems is permitted. Assimilation is not only a myth; it is also a sin. Furthermore, any combat on behalf of a nation-state, even a Muslim state, contributes to the destruction of the Muslim community. It is an obligation to fight for the *umma* and not for the nation, whether the nation is Muslim or infidel. Hizb ul-Tahrir therefore champions the same ideas as Bin Laden, except that the term *'jihad'* is absent from its vocabulary. It scrupulously avoids all reference to armed struggle, and none of its militants has been convicted of acts of violence, which no doubt explains why it was not placed on the list of terrorist organisations in the wake of the first attack on the World Trade Centre. However, Hizb ul-Tahrir is certainly one of those movements bound to attract attention in the future, whether it turns to violent action or serves as a focus for the politicisation of those who themselves take up violence.

Hizb ul-Tahrir is a genuinely internationalist movement, to the extent that it is difficult to identify and locate precisely its controlling authority. Officially its leader is Sheikh Abdel Qadir Zalum, a Palestinian settled in Beirut who in 1977 succeeded Nabhani, the founding father. In fact, it appears that Zalum is no longer the real leader of the organisation, which seems actually to be under the control of a group of militants based in London. A further puzzle relates to the relationship between Hizb ul-Tahrir and the Muhajirun organisation of Sheikh Omar Bakri, a Syrian resident in London who maintains a high profile in the English-language media. Although Bakri does not refer explicitly to Hizb ul-Tahrir, his pronouncements and his websites are often identical. Thus it seems that the Muhajirun movement, may be regarded as a front for Hizb ul-Tahrir, which essentially developed in the 1980s and '90s in Western Europe–Britain, the Netherlands and Sweden—and to a lesser extent in the United States, though appearing for the moment to be unknown in France. However, from 1997 it established chapters in Muslim countries, including Sudan, Uzbekistan and Pakistan. The Pakistani branch, led by Dr Abdul Qayyum, is more recent than the Uzbek branch, set up in 1999—and was also more visible, with its meetings even announced in the press. However, at the end of October 2001 after its first demonstration the police sealed its office. The Hizb ul-Tahrir has had little impact in Pakistan; it seems to have been set up at the instance of London and its members are mostly Pakistani expatriates. Its official spokesman, Naveed Butt, is an electrical engineer who graduated from the University of Chicago.

Hizb ul-Tahrir distinguishes itself carefully from other movements based in Afghanistan. However, according to the Kyrgyz security services, Hizb ul-Tahrir literature has been found in the possession of fighters of the Islamic Movement of Uzbekistan. The same sources indicate that Hizb ul-Tahrir is said to have sent emissaries to Kabul in September 2000. These allegations must, of course, be accepted with caution. However, it is highly probable that a certain number of IMU militants or sympathisers joined Hizb ul-Tahrir as the result of being discontented with the IMU's provincialism and strict militarism. The military defeat of the movement in Afghanistan, the death of Namangani and its suppression in Uzbekistan will no doubt accelerate the transfer of IMU militants to Hizb ul-Tahrir, even if its field of recruitment are not the same: Hizb ul-Tahrir's recruits are younger and better educated.

3. Afghanistan: from the Islamists to the Taliban and Al-Qaida

In Afghanistan the two historic Islamic parties, Hizb-i-Islami and Jami'at-i-Islami,[1] both of which had close relations in the 1970s with the Pakistani Jamaat-i-Islami, evolved very differently. The Hizb, led by Gulbuddin Hekmatyar, was an instrument of Pakistani influence up to 1994. Maintaining a strongly Islamist and even anti-American line, it quarrelled with its Saudi patron at the time of the Gulf War in 1991. As a result of the rise of the Taliban in 1994 it lost what remained of its base in Afghanistan, since the Pushtuns and the radicals rallied to the Taliban, while the Taliban also became the beneficiary of Pakistani aid. Having fled to Iran, Hekmatyar continued to press his case, but found himself totally isolated after being expelled from Iran in February 2002, and even became the target of an assassination attempt by the American armed forces.

The Jami'at, by contrast, followed a trajectory of the same kind as the Tajik Party of the Islamic Renaissance. Abandoning its ideological pretensions in 1987, it thereafter presented itself as an Afghan nationalist party, although its base remained quite narrowly ethnic, being located among the Persian-speaking Sunnis of the north. It constituted the essential element of the United Front (the Northern Alliance), which drew together the opponents of the Taliban, and profited substantially from the aftermath of 11 September. However, its principal leader, Massoud, was assassinated on 9 September 2001. It was in fact Massoud's troops who captured Kabul on 13 November.

[1] Cf. Olivier Roy, *Afghanistan, islam et modernité politique*, Paris: Le Seuil, 1985

True Islamic activism in Afghanistan was represented after 1992 by the Taliban movement and by the Arab volunteers located in the country. The Taliban recruited mainly among the students of a network of rural and Pushtun religious schools (*madrasas*), situated between Ghazni and Kandahar, which had been linked since well before the war against the Soviet Union with a parent network based in Pakistan, and organised by the Deobandi school. These *madrasas* had become politicised and militarised during the war, but were linked at that time to the centrist conservative parties of the Afghan resistance, Nabi Muhammadi's Harakat-i-Inqilab-i-Islami (Islamic Revolutionary Movement) and the Hizb-i-Islami of Yunis Khalis. During the war the links with the Pakistani *madrasas* were strengthened. Afghan Taliban studied in Pakistan, Afghan refugees enrolled in Pakistani *madrasas*, and Pakistani volunteers joined the Afghans. Meanwhile the curriculum of instruction was 'wahhabised' under the influence of Saudi benefactors, and teaching that drew on traditional Muslim culture in philosophy, poetry and the teaching of the Persian language were allowed to lapse. In 1994 these networks achieved autonomy, and were transmuted into a politico-religious movement under the direction of a charismatic young leader, Mullah Omar, with the direct support of the Pakistani authorities. It was they who took Kabul in 1996. At the outset the Taliban was not at all anti-Western, and its victory was hailed by the US State Department. However, it underwent a neo-fundamentalist radicalisation under Bin Laden's influence. This involved the strict application of Shari'a, the banning of women from public activity, and destruction of statues of the Buddha. Then, still under Bin Laden's influence, this radicalisation took on an increasingly anti-Western aspect following the United Nations sanctions.

The nature of the Taliban movement was twofold. On the one hand it was a puritan religious movement, of a fundamentalist and rigorous nature, but with no political project beyond "the Shari'a, the whole Shari'a, and nothing but the Shari'a". Taliban Islam in this sense displayed a Saudi character and did not relate to an anti-imperialist revolutionary project, such as had previously existed in Iran and prevails today under Bin Laden. On the other hand, it was also a movement sustained by a Pushtun nationalism which sought to re-establish the Afghan state, the traditional fief of the Pushtuns which was "appropriated" in 1992 by the Northern Alliance under the command of Massoud. The Shari'a was a means towards the construction of such a state, since it allowed the setting aside of tribal divisions and, to a lesser extent, ethnic distinctions. From this arose the substantial efforts made by the Taliban to obtain international recognition. However, once they had become convinced that their efforts, particularly those aimed at suppressing the cultivation of the opium poppy, were not being recognised by the international community, they increasingly fell in line with the anti-Western stance of their Pakistani patrons.

Although the Taliban had no objectives outside the frontiers of Afghanistan, they provided space within their territory for training camps for foreign volunteers and made use of units made up of such volunteers in their military campaigns. The international militant connections of the Taliban have been constructed around two other focuses, namely the al-Qaida organisation based in Kandahar in Afghanistan, and the Pakistani networks based around Lahore.

Al-Qaida's implantation in Afghanistan dates back to the days following the Soviet invasion. In 1983, under the aegis of Prince Turki, the Saudi minister of information, and of the Pakistani secret services (ISI), and with the approval of the CIA, a plan was put into operation to transfer Islamic volunteers to Afghanistan. In charge of the operation was Abdullah Azzam, a Palestinian Muslim Brother from Jenin, a doctoral graduate in Shari'a of Al-Azhar who had taught at the King Abdul Aziz University at Jedda, where in the late 1970s Bin Laden had been his pupil. Abdullah Azzam was in addition an official in the educational department of the World Islamic League, and had also taught at the Islamic University in Islamabad. In 1984 he moved to Peshawar where he founded the

Maktab ul-Khadamat (Services Office) for the *mujahidin*. He was a theoretician of the Afghan *jihad* and the intellectual mentor of Osama Bin Laden, who financed him initially from his own resources, and served as a recruiting agent. However, Azzam was assassinated in Peshawar in November 1989.[2] The militants co-operated in principle with Gulbuddin Hekmatyar's Hizb-i-Islami. These first-generation volunteers were mainly Arabs from the Middle East who had come to Afghanistan in order to fight against the Soviets. Once in Afghanistan, the Services Office generally divided them up into small groups, but from 1987 onwards they formed entire operational units based in the provinces of Paktia and Nangrahar, fighting in the regions of Khost and Jalalabad. A report compiled for Osama Bin Laden provides the following information: "A total of 2,359 young men from eight Arab countries have died in the course of the *jihad* in Afghanistan. Among these martyrs 433 were from Saudi Arabia, 526 from Egypt, 184 from Iraq, 284 from Libya, 180 from Syria, 540 from Algeria, 111 from Sudan and 100 from Tunisia."[3]

The hard core of the Arabs became established in 1986 in a special camp near Khost called *Masada* (the lion's den), and it was here that the international group came into being. This camp was attacked in 1987 by the Russians. Among the partici-pants in the battle were Bin Laden; Hassan Abdel Rab el-Saray (or el-Sarihi), a thirty-five-year-old Saudi, who was to carry out the attack in Riyadh in November 1995; Abu Zubayr Madani, who was killed in Bosnia in 1992; Khattab, who was to be seen again in Chechnya; and Sheikh Tamim Adnani, one of whose sons was killed with Azzam in November 1989. This battle could to an extent be viewed as the operation which saw the foundation of al-Qaida. At the point in February 1989 when the Americans were backing out as the Soviets withdrew,

---

[2] A deed for which some hold Bin Laden himself responsible. Cf. Rohan Gunaratna, *Inside Al-Qaeda*, London: Hurst, 2002.

[3] Imtiaz Hussein, "Usama prepares a list of Arab martyrs of Afghan Jihad", *The Frontier Post*, 13 May 2000.

these militants played a key role in attempting to bring Hekmatyar to power on behalf of the Pakistanis. They failed, and it was Massoud who took Kabul in May 1992.

Differences between Abdullah Azzam and Bin Laden emerged around 1987. Abdullah Azzam placed the emphasis on the Afghan *jihad* and refused to be drawn into inter-Afghan quarrels. He visited Massoud two months before his death. Bin Laden, on the other hand, was more internationalist and supported the radical Afghans, which at the time meant Hekmatyar. When Azzam was assassinated in November 1989, his natural successor—his son-in-law, the Algerian Bounoua—was sidelined in favour of Bin Laden. It is not clear whether Bin Laden immediately transformed the "Services Office" into al-Qaida. However, the movement wavered. The departure of the Soviets and the defeat of the Islamic forces before Jalalabad in the spring of 1989, followed by the Gulf War and the independence of the Soviet Republics, were all factors which confused the scene. The Saudis kept their distance from Hekmatyar, while many militants went back to their home countries to launch Islamic campaigns, except for the Egyptians who were still being actively sought out by the authorities in Cairo. Bin Laden himself left Afghanistan in 1990 and went to Saudi Arabia to try to persuade the monarchy not to solicit American support against Saddam Hussein. He then appeared in Somalia, where he seems to have participated in actions against American troops from 1992 to 1994. He was seen later in Yemen, and finally in Sudan from where he was expelled in 1996. He then returned to Jalalabad, which was still under the control of Hajji Qadir (subsequently governor of the city, and assassinated in 2002), Massoud's ally. Bin Laden travelled with Aryana Airlines, then under the control of Massoud's supporters, to whom he was introduced by the Pakistani intelligence services after the Taliban took Jalalabad without a fight in September 1996.

The Gulf War of 1991 and the disappearance of the Soviet Union played a considerable part in radicalising the organisation. From this point on, the Islamic militants took the view that their principal enemy was the United States. Many went back to establish radical movements at home, such as the Islamic Salvation Front and the Armed Islamic Group, while an internationalist faction undertook anti-American operations, including the attack on the World Trade Centre in February 1993. It was thus that a Bin Laden tendency came into being, its principal objective being the struggle against the United States, which saw Afghanistan as a sanctuary rather than as the model of the society which it wished to construct.

The militants who went back to their own countries quickly made their reputation. In Algeria those who took their places in the ranks of the FIS included Said Mekhloufi (founder of the MEI), Kamareddine Kherbane, a former fighter pilot; and Abdallah Anas, born in 1948, who under his real name Boudjema Bounoua arrived in Afghanistan in 1984. He was the son-in-law of Abdullah Azzam. However, they mainly rallied to the GIA, all of whose earliest leaders were "Afghans".[4] These included Tayyeb al-Afghani, who was killed in November 1992; Jaffar al-Afghani, killed in March 1994, and Sherif Gousmi, killed in September 1994. The ideologues of the London-based GIA journal *al-Ansar*, the Syrian Abu Messaab and the Egyptian Abu Hamza al-Masri, whose real name was Mustafa Kamel, had also lived in Peshawar. Abu Hamza, who became the *imam* of the Finsbury Park mosque in London, had also lost both hands and an eye while fighting the Soviets. His mosque became a prime focus of Islamic activity and seemingly a recruitment centre for young men who were to go to Afghanistan. From Egypt Mohammed al-Islambouli, the brother of Sadat's assassin, also found his way to Peshawar. Ayman al-Zawahiri, the leader of the Egyptian Jihad, was another veteran of Afghanistan, where he installed himself with Bin Laden in 1996, as did Fuad Qassim and Ahmed Taha, the heads of Al-Gamaat al-Islamiyya. In Jordan another of Bin Laden's associates, Muhammad Khalifa, was found guilty in a trial and condemned for

---

[4] As the veterans who had fought in Afghanistan were described.

conspiracy in 1998. In the Philippines the Janjalani brothers founded the Abu Sayyaf movement, a splinter group of the Moros Muslim autonomy movement, supported up to the time of writing by Libya. In Kashmir former fighters from Afghanistan joined the Harakat ul-Ansar. In Chechnya Khattab launched the offensive in the autumn of 1999. Mohammed Sadiq Odeh, a Palestinian born in Saudi Arabia, received his training at Khost in 1990 before being sent to New York to prepare the 1993 attack on the World Trade Centre. In Yemen Sheikh Tariq al-Fadli and Zein al-Abdine Abu Bakr al-Mihdar founded, respectively, Islamic Jihad and the Islamic Army of Aden al-Abyan, at the beginning of the 1990s.

The militants who went to Afghanistan were far from being entirely hotheads. Indeed, the assassination of Abdullah Azzam took place when he was preparing to transfer his allegiance to the most moderate of the *mujahidin*. In addition the Algerian Abdullah Anas, who strongly condemned the atrocities of the GIA, was a contender against Bin Laden for the succession to Abdullah Azzam. All the same, the network which took shape in Afghanistan from 1996 under Bin Laden promoted a violent jihadism which found enthusiastic followers in Pakistan towards the end of the 1990s.

4. Pakistan: from Religious Conservatism to Political Radicalism

The situation in Pakistan is much more complex. Since the 1990s movements and acronyms have arisen in profusion. In the background there are two clear distinctions to be made. First, there is the division based on ethnicity, which is mainly between Sindhis, Baluchis and Muhajirs, on the one hand, and Punjabis and Pushtuns on the other. In the conflicts between individuals it is important not to overlook caste loyalties which, while not publicly acknowledged, play an important role. Second, and principally, there is the religious divide which places the Shi'ites, who make up 15–20 per cent of the population, in opposition to the Sunnis. In addition, within the Sunni population, the Deobandis,—who are reformists drawn mainly from the Muhajirs, the Punjabis and the Pushtuns are opposed to the Barelvis, traditionalists who venerate saints and the Prophet. The latter are in the majority in the country. Meanwhile a third religious group characterised as "*wahhabi*" is antagonistic to these other two.

The religious movements have undergone two different forms of radicalisation: Islamist and neo-fundamentalist. The prototype of the Islamist party is the Jamaat-i-Islami, founded by Maulana Maududi in the 1940s, and up till the 1980s it enjoyed a virtual monopoly of political Islam and served as the link between the Pakistani army and the pro-Pakistan Afghan *mujahidin* of Gulbuddin Hekmatyar's Hizb-i-Islami. This came about in particular as a result of the role played by Qazi Hussein Ahmad, the party's "*emir*", who is himself a Pakistani Pushtun and in the early 1970s kept a tutelary eye on the young Afghan militants, including Hekmatyar and Massoud when these two were political refugees in Peshawar. Jamaat-i-Islami recruited mainly among intellectuals with a modern education, and maintained its distance from pre-existing clerical and religious movements. It has always respected the rule of law, in spite of its ideological radicalism which declared Pakistan's status as an Islamic state to be the sole reason for its existence. It was also élitist, advocating "entryism" into the senior civil service and the army, and has never undertaken armed action. It lost impetus after 1991, and its former position is occupied today by a radical tendency which has arisen out of other movements which were initially more conservative.

Jamaat has never been included in the roster of terrorist parties drawn up by the United States government. On the other hand, it developed into an Islamo-nationalist party—for example, at the time of the campaign against the signature of the non-proliferation treaty in 2000. No doubt it was attracted by the idea of becoming the civil alternative to the military regime of Musharraf, who came to power in October 1999. However, the American campaign of 2001 placed it once more in the dissident camp, although it had not gone so far as to enter the armed conflict. Jamaat seems to have opted definitively for the political route.

The principal formative influence of this new radicalism, coming from a conservative background, has been the Deobandi school, named after Deoband, a great religious academy founded near Delhi in 1867. It is made up of religious figures of a traditional and conservative inclination, whose manifestation in the sphere of politics is the Jamiat-i-Ulema-i-Islam, the largest Deobandi-based party, established in 1945, of which the two principal factions today are led by Maulana Fazlur Rehman and Maulana Sami Ul-Haq. Also located in this neo-fundamentalist orbit is the Ahl-i-Hadith, founded in the nineteenth century, whose adherents distinguish themselves from the Deobandis by their refusal to accept theological and philosophical thinking which has accrued in the course of Muslim history. In this sense they are close to the Saudi Wahhabis, and are often so described by their enemies. In 1987 members of the Ahl-i-Hadith, in the course of a process of radicalisation similar to that of other groups, set up the group Da'wa wa'l-Irshad (Preaching and Guidance), which has become their militant branch.

The Barelvi movement—counterpart and rival of the Deobandi school—has developed a more popular Islam, strongly focused on the Prophet Muhammad, and is often viewed by the Salafi and Wahhabi tendencies as having deviated from the true faith. However, the Barelvis are scarcely involved in Afghanistan, and promote their international networks only in Europe among the migrants from the Indian sub-continent.

The various religious movements—Deobandism, Barelvism and Ahl-i-Hadith—have no tradition of political radicalism. Even though they are strongly sectarian when religion is at issue, this always relates to specific problems, for example the condemnation of the Ahmadi movement or the campaign against Shi'ism, which is regarded as a heresy, and they do not militate for some particular form of government. These are very conservative movements, even when like the Deobandis and the Ahl-i-Hadith, they profess their adherence to religious reformism. Their transition into politics dates from the 1980s, and has taken the form of a growing radicalism and the adoption of violent action. This radicalisation has been characterised by the formation of armed splinter groups, often organised within a clandestine framework. It is therefore difficult to discover to what extent such groups are wholly autonomous or whether, on the other hand, their links to their parent organizations persist, although the acts of violence in which they engage may drive them further into clandestinity, especially after being listed in the various registers of terrorist organisations maintained by the United States.

This radicalisation of religious conservatives may also be observed elsewhere besides Pakistan, as in the case of the Taliban in Afghanistan. In Pakistan it is promoted by the military intelligence service, the ISI, and relates to two defined objectives.

These objectives are the struggle against Shi'ism, and the *jihad*, both in Kashmir and in Afghanistan. The objectives are not new but the means employed are novel. These include military training, the adoption of armed struggle, the assassination of individuals, and armed attacks on mosques of other persuasions. In addition there are strategic consequences. In Afghanistan, after the departure of the Soviets, *jihad* was waged against Massoud, both for the benefit of the Taliban and, with inexorable logic, also on behalf of al-Qaida which at that time had rallied these movements both against the United States and, after 11 September, against General Musharraf himself and the Pakistan army. Anti-Shi'ism and jihadism eventually coalesced.

Deobandi movements and violent action

The radicalisation of the Deobandi movements can be traced to the policy of conservative re-Islamisation instituted by General Zia ul-Haq after his seizure of power in Pakistan in 1977. It was afterwards nurtured by the hardening stance of the Pakistani state and of the radical movements which shared the same enemies—namely India, the communists and, to a lesser extent, the Shi'ites. However, the "militants" in due course turned to autonomous action and, while conserving their close connection with the services of the ISI, imposed their own strategy. The *jihad* in Afghanistan was both their model and, during the 1980s while it was still encouraged by the Saudis and the United States, their cover. The radical Islamic movements were therefore instruments for the regional policy of the Pakistani authorities and in particular for the ISI. The concern of the government over the uncontrollable spread of violence between Sunnis and Shi'ites led to the beginnings of a change of policy under the government of Nawaz Sharif in 1998, though without real results. In 1999 the new head of state General Musharraf embarked on the repression of the most sectarian movements while continuing to utilise some of them—for instance the Lashkar-i-Taiba—in Kashmir and Afghanistan. The impact of "sectarian conflict", an expression used to designate Sunni-Shi'ite tension, is frequently misunderstood and demands re-evaluation.[1]

Radicalisation in the internal sphere in Pakistan was undertaken as a stratagem against the Shi'ites in 1985, at a time when the Pakistani authorities feared that the Shi'ite community might be utilised by Iran's Islamic Revolution. Thus a number of movements of Deobandi sectarian character appeared, with the blessing of the authorities.

The Sipah-i-Sahaba Pakistan (SSP—the Army of the Companions of the Prophet) emerged from the Jami'at-i-Ulema-i-Islam, which professes to be in agreement with the SSP over ideology but not over methods. However, there has been no explicit break between these two parties, and hence their relationship is ambiguous. The SSP was founded in September 1985 at Jhang, with the backing of the military authorities, to counter the rise in the influence of Shi'ism, and apparently had the financial support of Saudi Arabia and Iraq. The principal objective of the SSP was to affirm the apostasy of the Shi'ites and to transform Pakistan into a Sunni Muslim state applying the Shari'a. The SSP was anti-Barelvi and strongly anti-Iranian, and accused the Pakistan government of conducting repression against the Sunnis with the aim of gratifying Iran. It demanded the enactment of a law imposing the death penalty for any slur on the honour of the *sahaba*, the companions of the Prophet, or of Aisha, the Prophet's wife. This specifically implied condemnation of the Shi'ite ritual, which disapproves of both Aisha and the Caliph Omar. The assassination in February 1990 of the movement's founder Haq Nawaz Jhangvi unleashed a cycle of inter-communal violence which continued through December 1990 with the assassination in Lahore of the consul-general of Iran, Sadiq Ganji. The assassin, who had taken the

---

[1] Cf. S. V. R. Nasr, "Islam, the State and the Rise of Sectarian Militancy in Pakistan" in C. Jaffrelot, ed., *Pakistan, nationalism without a Nation?*, London: Zed Books, 2002, pp. 85–114.

name Haq Nawaz, was condemned to death and hanged in February 2001. The successors of Haq Nawaz Jhangvi were also murdered—Maulana Isar ul-Qasmi in 1991 and Zia ul-Rehman Farooqi in 1997.

The last leader of the SSP was Maulana Azam Tariq, a Punjabi whose family left the Indian Punjab for Pakistan in 1947. In addition to Jhang, the areas of the SSP's strength were in the centre of the country, around Faisalabad, and in the southern Punjab including Bahawalpur, Multan, Muzaffargarh and Rahimyar Khan. Its support came from the Sunni and Deobandi urban lower middle class, merchants and junior officials from the Punjabi and Muhajir communities. It continued to receive financial backing principally from private Saudi sources, as well as from the Punjabi diaspora, in Europe and even more in the Middle East, and from the Islamic *zakat* tax. It may well also have been supported by the (internal) transport cartels and drug-trafficking mafias.

The SSP, which claimed to be a religious rather than a political party, made an entry into electoral politics in its own right in 1992, its candidates having previously stood for election under the banner of the Jami'at-i-Ulema-i-Islam. It won seats in the National Assembly and in the Provincial Assembly of the Punjab. Under Benazir Bhutto's second government, from 1993 to 1996, Sipah-i-Sahaba entered an alliance with the Pakistan People's Party (PPP) in the Punjab and secured a ministerial post in the provincial government. The SSP claimed to have 300,000 members, and to be especially well represented in the Punjab and in Punjabi circles in Karachi. It recruited largely from the Deobandi *madrasas* of the Punjab. It has maintained offices abroad, in the United Arab Emirates, Saudi Arabia, Canada, Britain and Bangladesh among others. Its leader Azam Tariq visited France in January 2001, shortly before he was once again placed in detention on 27 February 2001 after the disturbances which followed the hanging of Haq Nawaz. At the end of the 1990s the SSP fought alongside the Taliban against Massoud and the Afghan Shi'ite Hazaras, and is thought to have been responsible for the massacre of Hazaras and Iranian diplomats in northern Afghanistan in August 1998. It was banned on 12 January 2002.

Azam Tariq was first placed under house arrest, although the authorities granted him a monthly allowance of 10,000 rupees. He contested and won a parliamentary seat in the October 2002 election as an independent candidate, although he faced about sixty criminal cases including murder, inciting people to commit sectarian violence and making hate speeches. He challenged the ban on his group by filing a petition in the Supreme Court. The defunct SSP, which took the new name of Millat-e Islamia Party (MIP, Party of the Islamic Nation), spared no effort to become acceptable to the government. Azam Tariq insisted that his party was purely a religio-political one whose sole aim was the implementation of sharia laws, and that it had no links to the *jihadi* or sectarian groups. In April 2003 he appealed to the Lahore High Court to suspend the state orders freezing his party's bank accounts and imposing functional restrictions on it, claiming that these orders had brought its social and humanitarian work to a halt and affected its religious functions since hundreds of mosques drew funds for their maintenance from the party's coffers. Although Azam Tariq denied it, there is every reason to believe that his release and his election to the National Assembly were the result of a deal with the government which apparently wanted to use him to undermine the Muttahida Majlis-e Amal (MMA, United Action Council), the alliance of six religious parties which has been at the forefront of the opposition to General Musharraf since its success in the October 2002 elections. Azam Tariq was assassinated in Islamabad on 6 October 2003. Meanwhile, the SSP which had been declared a terrorist organization by Pakistan in December 2001, was placed on a terrorist watchlist by the United States in May 2003. Inside Pakistan itself, incidents of sectarian violence perpetrated by Sunnis have always tended more to be the work of the Lashkar-i-Jhangvi (LJ—Army of Jhangvi).

The latter, a terrorist group, split off in 1994 from the SSP, which it accused of having abandoned the agenda laid down by Haq Nawaz Jhangvi. It was led by Riaz Basra, an SSP veteran from Sarghoda, who is said to have lived in Kabul till October 2001 and was accused of implication in the assassination of Sadiq Ganji. Malik Ishaq, the ideologue of the LJ, has been in prison since 1998. This is a very decentralised and compartmentalised group, and until the autumn of 2001 it numbered several dozen dedicated assassins based in Afghanistan. It has claimed responsibility for numerous assassinations, the victims including Iranian diplomats and military personnel, high-ranking police officers, senior officials, lawyers, doctors and Shi'ite preachers. The organisation has also carried out massacres at Shi'ite mosques. It drew up a death-list of Shi'ite personalities and even attempted to kill the Prime Minister, Nawaz Sharif, in January 1999 in reprisal for the oppressive campaign carried out in the Punjab in 1998 by Shahbaz Sharif, the brother of Nawaz, who was the provincial Chief Minister. The LJ was proscribed in August 2002. Riaz Basra was arrested in December 2001 on his return from Afghanistan and executed extra-judicially by the police on May 2002 in a false encounter, two days before the recovery of the dead body of Daniel Pearl was announced. He had always been suspected of collaborating with the agencies since his "escape" from jail in Lahore in 1994 after which he created the Lashkar-e Jhangvi.

The active jihadist tendency in Kashmir and Afghanistan: from the Harakat ul-Ansar to the Jaish-i-Muhammad

The Soviet invasion of Afghanistan imparted a new dimension to the idea of *jihad* in Pakistan, which till then had only been employed by the Pakistani state in the context of mobilising the population against India. However, from the beginning of the 1980s the concept of *jihad* was to become 'privatised'. Radical groups emerged out of the large traditional religious movements and embarked on armed operations.

There are three elements which serve to explain the complexity of the process of radicalisation, and in particular the multiplication of small groups of terrorists. The latter often occurs through a process of larger groups becoming subdivided. The first of these elements is that such movements arose from the initiative of young militants who had personally experienced *jihad* while fighting in Kashmir or Afghanistan. The second is that the development of these movements was supervised by the Pakistani secret services (ISI), which had two objectives in view—to take control of the *jihad* in Kashmir by marginalising their nationalist elements to the benefit of the "Islamic internationalists", based in Pakistan and reporting directly to the ISI, and to intervene in internal Pakistani politics, in particular against the Shi'ites who were suspected of serving as a fifth column for a hypothetical Iranian infiltration. And the third is that the rise of such movements was discreetly overseen by the great politico-religious organizations, which were thus able to furnish themselves with an armed branch while at the same time being able to deny all responsibility if a serious crisis had arisen.

The first genuine Pakistani jihadist movement is said to have been founded in 1980.[2] Three students from the large Deobandi *madrasa* (Jamiat ul Ulum ul Islamia) at Binori Town in Karachi left for Afghanistan in February 1980, without money and not knowing what they intended to do there. They gave their group the name Jami'at ul-Ansar of Afghanistan (Society of the Partisans), which in 1988 became Harakat ul-Jihad-i-Islami (HJI). When the three students arrived in Peshawar they joined the Harakat-i-Inqilab-e-Islami, the radical extremist faction of Maulvi Nasrullah Mansur, which was well established in the Afghan province of Paktia (close to the Pakistan border) and was run by traditional clergy educated in Pakistan. They were also connected to the Hizb-i-Islami of Yunus

---

[2] Nevertheless, a precursor to Pakistani jihadism was Massoud Alvi, who in 1973 founded the Jabha-Khalidia at Khair ul-Madaris in Multan, where he taught. Fazlur Rehman Khalil, founder of the Harakat ul-Ansar, was his student. This movement became the international Jami'at ul-Mujahidin during the Afghan *jihad*.

Khalis and to Jalaluddin Haqqani, who would become one of the senior local commanders of the Taliban.

The HJI was pan-Islamic, and its intention was, by means of a renewed *jihad*, to combat the worldwide oppression of Muslims by infidels. Its objective was to give the Muslims back their past glory, and it placed special emphasis on the liberation of occupied Muslim territory such as Kashmir and Palestine. It also aimed at launching a struggle for Muslim rights in non-Muslim countries, such as the Philippines and Burma. In due course its activists fought in Bosnia, where a first group arrived in 1992, and in Tajikistan—as well as in other places. However, from 1980 to 1988 it restricted its activities to Afghanistan. A split took place in 1991, resulting in the formation of a movement called the Harakat ul-Ansar (HUA), later known as the Harakat ul-Mujahidin (HUM). The leading figure in this group, Fazlur Rehman Khalil, a Pushtun, had great influence, and numerous militants rallied to him. The Harakat ul-Mujahidin (HUM), led by Fazlur Rehman Khalil and Masood Azhar, featured on an early list of terrorist organisations drawn up by the US State Department in 1998. This movement devoted itself primarily to the struggle in Kashmir, where Masood Azhar was taken prisoner by India in 1994. In February 2000 a new split followed, apparently along ethnic lines. The Punjabi militants followed Masood Azhar into the Jaish-i-Mohammad (JM—the Army of Mohammed), as the new group was named, while the Pushtuns remained with Fazlur Rehman Khalil in the HM, which henceforth became an essentially Pushtun movement allied to Bin Laden with camps in Afghanistan.

Here a pattern is observable which was to repeat itself with other movements, namely that religious and ethnic connections reinforced each other. Recruitment for the new group was conducted mainly among the veterans of Sipah-i-Sahaba Pakistan, the Punjabis of the Harakat ul-Mujahidin, and the Kashmiri and Punjabi communities in Britain.

The founding of the Jaish-i-Muhammad (JM, Army of Muhammad) in Karachi in February 2000 followed the hijacking of an Indian Airlines plane at Kandahar airport in December 1999, which led to the release of Masood Azhar by the Indian authorities. He was subsequently re-arrested and released twice by Pakistan in February and April 2000 because of his over-vigorous criticism of the Musharraf government. However, he retained the backing of the Pakistani secret service (ISI) and continued to go about armed in public. Shortly after the launch of the Jaish-i-Muhammad he went back to Bahawalpur, where he married before setting off again for Afghanistan. The Jaish-i-Muhammad and its founder merit close examination, since it undoubtedly became the most active jihadist movement and the closest to al-Qaida.

Masood Azhar was born in 1968 at Bahawalpur into a religious family of six sons and six daughters. His father was an instructor in Islamic studies. He was intellectually able, so his father sent him to the major Deobandi *madrasa* at Binori Town in Karachi, where he studied from 1980 to 1989. He afterwards lectured in Arabic at Binori Town to foreign students for two years. A visit by a leader of the Harakat ul-Ansar prompted the principal of the *madrasa* there to suggest to Masood Azhar that he should follow a course of preparation for the *jihad*. He returned converted to the necessity for action. Appointed by the Harakat ul-Ansar in 1993 to be responsible for *da'wa*, he published the periodicals *Sada ul-Mujahidin* (Voice of the Mujahidin) in Urdu, and *Sawt ul-Kashmir* (Voice of Kashmir) in Arabic.

He went to Afghanistan with his brother Ibrahim Azhar, a madrasa graduate and former amir of the Bahawalpur chapter of the Harakat ul Ansar, who was one of the hijackers of the Indian Airlines plane in December 1999. Ibrahim lives in Karachi and runs the Idara Khairul Amin, an organisation based in Binori Town which prints *jihadi* literature. His younger brother, Abdul Rauf Asghar, also studied at Binori Town, and later joined the *madrasa* as a teacher. Two younger brothers are currently studying at Deobandi *madrasas* in Karachi. Masood Azhar entered India from Bangladesh on a forged Portuguese passport in 1994 and was captured by the Indians in Kashmir. During his detention in India, he wrote numerous articles and works on the *jihad*, often referring in these writings to Africa, he is said by some to have followed Bin Laden to Sudan in 1992, and to have fought in Somalia for the local warlord Aidid. He is also said to have been involved in the training of militants in Yemen.

After the seizure of power by General Musharraf, Masood Azhar hailed the fall of the tyrannical regime of Nawaz Sharif and demanded reforms, including an Islamic constitution that would proclaim the supremacy of the Quran and the Sunna. He also proposed a revision of the electoral system so that only good Muslims ready to make the greatest sacrifices for Islam could be candidates, as well as the Islamisation of the judicial system and of the economy, with the abolition of interest-bearing loans. He named the internal enemies of Pakistan: the politicians who had pillaged the country and left it in debt; the feudal landowners who had appropriated lands and oppressed the peasants; corrupt officials; merchants who sold sub-standard goods and operated on the black market; organizations which drew distinctions between Muslims on the basis of their ethnicity or language; those who wished to transform Pakistan into an American or Russian colony; the majority of foreign-controlled NGOs, which he regarded as ideological enemies of Pakistan whose personnel were mainly in the pay of the "Jewish lobby"; writers and journalists who undermined the unity and security of the country, exploiting their right of freedom of expression to write against Islam—he accused them of responsibility for sectarianism, and alleged that they were supported from abroad; and finally those who disseminated obscenity and promoted an atmosphere of sinfulness.

Masood Azhar was very close to the Sipah-i-Sahaba-Pakistan and to Maulana Azam Tariq. In fact the SSP, the JM and the Lashkar-e Jhangvi appeared to be three wings of the same party: the SSP was a political umbrella while the JM and the Lashkar-e Jhangvi were the *jihadi* and domestic military wings respectively.

A rumour which circulated in 2001 concerning a possible ban on the SSP was a further factor leading to the adherence of a number of its members to the Jaish-i Muhammad, although in fact only the Lashkar-i-Jhangvi was definitively banned, in August 2001. Soon after its creation the JM became involved in sectarian warfare in Pakistan in addition to its activities in Kashmir. A faction of the JM, led by Abdul Jabbar, carried out sectarian attacks in Islamabad's diplomatic enclave on a Christian church frequented by Americans in March 2002, and on a Shia mosque in Punjab in April 2002. His arrest for these specific attacks was announced in early July 2003. He is also said to have been behind the Taxila attack on a Christian hospital in August 2002. It so happened that the members of the JM had exactly the same profile as those of the SSP, since it recruited from the rural and urban lower middle class and from the *madrasas*. The JM recruited also in Britain among emigrant Kashmiris and Punjabis. The JM militant who on 25 December 2000 drove a car full of explosives into an Indian army base was a young man from Birmingham, Mohammed Bilal (alias Asif), who had converted to Islam after a having a vision of the Prophet Muhammad in a dream. This suicide attack was typical of the methods of Jaish-i Muhammad, which was one of the first jihadist groups in South Asia to import the technique of suicide missions from the Middle East. The JM also carried out a number of attacks against the Indian forces in Srinagar in April 2000.

The Jaish-i-Mohammad was banned in January 2002. Masood Azhar had renamed his party Tehrik al Furqan in December 2001 after the US State Department had expressed concern about the "terrorist" activities of the JM. After the ban of the JM he was placed under house arrest at Bahawalpur and the authorities granted him a monthly pension of 10,000 rupees. He was released by order of the court in December 2002 and has since kept a low profile. The JM has adopted the name of Tehrik Khuddam ul Islam (Movement of the servants of Islam). The new organisation split in June 2003 after violent clashes over control of a mosque in Karachi between rival factions led respectively by Masood Azhar and Abdullah Shah Mazar, the Karachi amir of the movement. The latter, who was expelled, formed his own faction.

Salafism and jihadism

The other jihadist movement which carried out comparable operations in Kashmir was the Lashkar-i-Taiba, an offshoot of the Markaz Da'wa wal Irshad (the Centre for Preaching and Guidance). The latter organisation, which was ideologically affiliated to the Wahhabi Ahl-i-Hadith, was set up in 1987 by Abdullah Azzam (see below), Hafez Saeed and Dr Zafar Iqbal (Abu Hamza). The latter two were educated in Saudi Arabia at the Islamic University in Medina. Hafez Saeed taught at the faculty of engineering and technology at the University of Lahore. The base for Da'wa wal Irshad was installed at Muridke, close to Lahore, on a 190-acre plot donated by the government of General Zia ul-Haq. On the site, in addition to the Um al-Qura mosque, was an educational complex which included a university, a farm, a clothing factory, and a carpentry workshop. The intention was to create a model town in a purely Islamic environment wholly removed from the authority of the Pakistani state. Da'wat wal Irshad received a substantial amount of Saudi aid in its early years, particularly from a certain Sheikh Abu Abdul Aziz, who some sources say was Osama Bin Laden himself. The movement was essentially financed by private Arab donors (Saudi philanthropists discontented with the way the Royal Family governed the kingdom), as well as by the Pakistani diaspora of merchants and traders in the Middle East and Europe, including Britain, the Netherlands and, according to certain sources, France. It also received local gifts in money and kind, and enjoyed revenue from the processing of the hides of the animals sacrificed during Id al-Adha (Feast of the Sacrifice), which were sold at auction.

Da'wa wal Irshad had two explicit objectives. One was *da'wa*—preaching—and this was coupled with education and *jihad,* which were regarded by the movement as inseparable and of equal importance. This was what endowed it with its particular character relative to the other jihadist movements. Hafez Saeed said in August 1999: "Da'wat and jihad are of an equal and inseparable importance.... Da'wat and jihad are basic and we cannot prefer one to the other.... If beliefs and morals are left unreformed, da'wa alone can lead to anarchy.... It is therefore necessary to fuse the two. This is the only way to transform individual human beings, society and the world."[3]

In the tradition of the reformist Sunni movements of the region, Da'wa wal Irshad seeks to purify society and South Asian Islam from Hindu influences. It appeals to the authority of Ibn Taymiyya, of Muhammad ibn Abd al-Wahhab and of Syed Ahmed Barelvi (Ahmed Shaheed) and Ismail Shaheed, the leaders of the so-called "Wahhabi" movement, who waged a *jihad* against the Sikhs in the 1820s and founded the Islamic emirate of Peshawar; Ahmed Shaheed is an authority turned to by most of the jihadist movements. In 1994 the movement set up a network of schools which spread rapidly throughout the entire country—especially, in recent years, in Sind, where it has purchased real estate. Arabic and English are taught in addition to the Quranic sciences,—the aim being not merely to purify society by the teaching of the Quran and the Sunna, i.e. to promote a Wahhabi version of Islam as distinct from popular Pakistani Islam, but also to prepare individuals to be receptive to the *da'wa,* to relate the faith to modern knowledge, and to teach children in such a way as to repair the damage done by secular education. The content of school texts is centred on the *jihad,* so that for example in the Urdu textbook for the second year of primary education there are the last testaments of *mujahidin* about to go into battle.

The schools, situated in the poorer quarters of the towns and in the villages of rural Sind, attract an increasing number of children. Their success is due to the weakness of state education,

[3] *Takbir,* August 1999

which has occasioned a proliferation of private establishments. These are often openly commercial enterprises of very mediocre quality, but they are attractive to families because they offer education through the medium of the English language. It is noteworthy that the religious parties have invested extensively in this sector, especially in the sphere of English teaching and information technology. The Da'wa wal Irshad schools, which boast a total of 140 establishments and 20,000 pupils, are concerned to attract a different clientele from that of the *madrasas*: They offer a more modern education better adapted to the labour market, and are now beginning to attract the lower middle class—people who cannot afford to pay the high tuition fees charged by good private schools.

Da'wa wal Irshad insists that while the activities of many Muslim organizations relate to *da'wa*, *jihad* has been neglected. In its view the present situation demands that Muslims devote themselves to *jihad*. This is to be directed against the Hindus, whom it regards as the worst polytheists, and against the Jews, who are singled out by the Quran as enemies and are also enemies of Pakistan, since (as they allege) Israel assists the Indian army in Kashmir. Like its radical counterparts, the movement offers a selective reading of those verses of the Quran which relate to Jews and Christians. It thus brings together the main pan-Islamic concerns. The activities of the movement are as a whole directed towards arousing a passion for *jihad* within individuals, as the only remedy for the range of evils to which Pakistani society is prone. It is particularly seen as a counter to sectarianism, as manifested by conflict between Sunnis and Shi'ites, and increasingly too between Deobandis and Barelvis, which is seen as yet one more conspiracy aimed at distracting Muslims from *jihad* against the infidels.

The armed wing of Da'wa wal-Irshad, the Lashkar-i-Taiba (LT—the Army of the Pure: *Taiba* is also an appelation of the holy city of Medina), has become the most active movement in Indian Kashmir, where it has supplanted both the nationalist Jammu and Kashmir Liberation Front and the Hizb ul-Mujahidin, linked to Jamaat-i-Islami. It has rapidly become notorious for its spectacular "missions impossible" such as the attacks on the airport at Srinagar and against Indian army barracks, such as that at Badami Bagh in November 1999. The attack in December 2000 against the Red Fort in Delhi was especially significant, since it symbolised the reconquest of the seat of the Moghul empire, occupied by the Hindus.[4]

The Lashkar-i-Taiba takes the position that in the absence of an Islamic state, the right to collect the *zakat* (the Islamic tax) has devolved upon it, and that it is entitled to wage *jihad* in any part of the world where Muslims are oppressed, that is to say not only in India but also in Palestine, Bosnia, Chechnya and the Philippines. The agenda of the Lashkar-i-Taiba is unambiguous: it intends to Islamise Kashmir and India, then embark on global conquest with the goal of restoring the Caliphate.

Hafez Saeed declares: "Our jihad will continue until Islam becomes the dominant religion.... Kashmir is no more than the gateway to India, and we shall strive also for the liberation of the 200 million Indian Muslims." Following the Soviet retreat from Afghanistan, the Lashkar-i-Taiba sent its *mujahidin* only to Kashmir, since the conflict in Afghanistan, where Muslims confront other Muslims, is in its eyes no longer an authentic *jihad*. It was banned in 2002, but till then in order to recruit volunteers it had set up a tightly-organised network throughout the country, with more than 2,000 local offices. Its militants were found throughout Pakistan, including the interior of Sind and Baluchistan. The monthly *Al-Dawat*, the most widely-read religious magazine in the Punjab, was printed in an edition of more than 80,000 copies and distributed through all possible outlets, notably in the English-language bookshops of the smart quarters of Islamabad and Karachi. The magazine reveals "the evils of society, in order to lead young people away from

---

[4] In addition a reconstruction was organised on the occasion of the Id al-Adha (the Feast of the Sacrifice) in Lahore's largest sports stadium with no reaction from the authorities, though all political assemblies were banned.

them". In addition to denouncing television, videocassettes and film music, it especially condemns Jewish conspiracies, the *qadiani* (the Ahmadi sect), and Barelvi practices which relate to the veneration of saints.

In contrast to other jihadist organizations which are active in Kashmir, 80 per cent of the combatants of the Lashkar-i-Taiba are Pakistani. The social profile of the *mujahidin* is identical to that of non-commissioned officers in the army, since recruitment is carried out—principally in the towns of the Punjab such as Gujranwala, Lahore and Multan,—among families of the lower middle class who, contrary to what is generally supposed, are not of Indian or Kashmiri origin. The majority of the *mujahidin* emerge from the Urdu-language system of public education, while only 10 per cent come from the *madrasas*. They are most frequently young town-dwellers who have left school without qualifications, and are either without work or are in low-paid employment which offers them poor prospects for the future. The Lashkar-i-Taiba has also made an effort to recruit in the universities and the high schools, since young men from the universities are more highly motivated and more aware of the significance of what they are undertaking. Young Pakistanis from Britain who join the Lashkar-i-Taiba are mainly university graduates and in skilled occupations. In the countryside the Lashkar-i-Taiba recruits from two social groups: families of Wahhabi inclination, who have often become converted to this school of thought after the head of the household has spent a period working in Saudi Arabia; and the poorer sections of society, since better-off and especially land-owning families do not send their sons to Kashmir. Finally, the Lashkar-i-Taiba takes in those who have been rejected by society; it makes considerable play of its rehabilitation of drug-addicts and petty criminals.

The annual gatherings of Dawat wal Irshad brought together more than 100,000 people at Muridke over a period of three days, and foreign delegates attended in addition to the *mujahidin* and the families of martyrs. There was much oratory on the themes of *jihad* and the restoration of the Caliphate, and the speeches were accessible on the movement's website. The *mujahidin* and the martyrs' families themselves also delivered impassioned addresses on the subject of *jihad*. Military displays were also mounted during the gatherings, and every year these produced hundreds of volunteers.

What motivated recruits to join Lashkar-i-Taiba? Every Pakistani youth is exposed from childhood to intense propaganda on the issue of Kashmir—at school, in the media and within the family. It is not hard to imagine the cumulative effect on an adolescent of the daily portrayal on television of powerful images of Indian troops maltreating Kashmiris, and of appalling tales of extortion and humiliation, often of a sexual nature, committed by Indian soldiers, who are frequently Sikhs, against the Muslim women of Kashmir. All this serves to re-ignite memories of the horrors of the partition of India in 1947, which are still of great significance in the collective memory of the Punjab and are often alluded to.

Nonetheless propaganda, however effective it may be—added to the desire to protect the honour of "their sisters and their mothers"—is not the only impetus driving young men to sign up with Lashkar-i-Taiba. Emigration, particularly to the Middle East, played the role of a safety valve between 1973 and 1986, after which it tailed off. It never in any case involved more than marginally either the southern Punjab or the poorest social classes, who were unable to muster the financial resources needed to fund emigration. People traffickers currently ask between 200,000 and 400,000 rupees for a departure to Europe, so that for the many Pakistanis who earn around 3,000–5,000 rupees a month travel abroad remains an inaccessible dream. However, the other safety valve for surplus workers is adherence to a religious party or jihadist movement which offers a degree of transformation of the individual's identity and some compensation for social frustrations, most of which stem from simple poverty. The political vacuum also contributes to the success of the *jihad*, since the Muslim League and the Pakistani

People's Party have failed, and the traditional religious parties are believed to be too willing to compromise, and to be no less corrupt than other political organizations.

Young men without a future therefore say "I want to be remembered as a martyr", just as they do in Palestine. Within Pakistani society, which is intensely hierarchical and focused on social status, and where social distinctions are increasingly marked, every individual strives to define his own status as superior in terms of either power, privilege or prestige. Under-achieving groups compensate for their inferiority in terms of power and privilege by adopting an ostentatious religiosity, and especially through the prestige which comes from participating in the *jihad* in Kashmir; this in turn reflects on all the family members of a combatant and even more on those of a martyr. In fact the family of a martyr acquires a privileged position, since it receives material benefits and often money. These considerations should not be under-rated, and they are especially relevant in the case of young men who were formerly unemployed, drug-addicts or petty criminals; their families might have been unable to cope with them but now, thanks to their sacrifice, they suddenly have a status which had previously seemed unattainable. Fathers have been heard to say "My son could have died of an overdose or in a traffic accident, or been killed by a thief in the street, but I have given him up voluntarily to be a martyr and to intercede with God on our behalf." On the other hand, a careful study of the socio-economic profile of martyrs has shown that some of them at least did not join Lashkar-i Taiba until after they had married and were in steady employment, as if they could not envisage the *jihad* until they had already achieved some of their personal objectives.

The earliest *mujahidin* of Lashkar-i-Taiba were trained in Afghanistan in the provinces of Paktia, where there was a camp at Jaji from 1987, and Kunar (Nuristan) with the Muaskar Taiba under the aegis of Maulana Jamil ul-Rahman. Afghans from Nuristan are fighting today in Kashmir in the ranks of the

Lashkar-i-Taiba, which maintains three training camps in Azad Kashmir, the part of Kashmir controlled by Pakistan. The principal one is Um al-Qura at Muzzaffarabad where 500 *mujahidin* are trained each month. The initial level of training, the basic course, lasts twenty-one days, candidates being selected by their local LT official who assesses their motivation. After this first session they go home and are kept under observation. They later take a further course lasting three weeks, devoted to religious indoctrination. Hafez Saeed was in the habit of saying that he would not put a weapon in the hands of any young recruit who had not first accepted a solid religious grounding, and who was not secure in his faith. If the candidates' behaviour at home appeared satisfactory—they were obliged to be model citizens and to have the general approval of those around them—they were allowed finally to take the three-month-long special course in the handling of light weapons, guerrilla tactics and survival techniques.

After completing this programme they returned home transformed. They kept their hair long, ceased to shave their beards, and wore their trousers short above their ankles. They also abandoned their own names and took the surname of a companion of the Prophet or a hero of the early days of Islam such as Abu Talha, Abi Huzaifa or Abu Hureira. A change of personality was in evidence. Militants themselves affirm that after the three-month course they were physically and mentally mature. This educational process therefore constituted a rite of passage. According to reliable sources, between 100,000 and 300,000 young men underwent military training. However, not all those go on to combat: many who receive training devote themselves to collecting funds or to propaganda, especially through the distribution of videocassettes of the atrocities committed in Kashmir. In any case, only those whose families give permission for them to go are sent to Kashmir, which implies that a process of persuading the relatives will be necessary when the latter have not themselves already accepted the Wahhabi ideology.

The Lashkar-i-Taiba adopted the strategy of suicide missions after the Kargil conflict between India and Pakistan in 1999. According to the supreme commander Maulana Zaki ul-Rehman Lakhvi, 891 Indian soldiers were killed in 2000 as a result of such attacks. Lashkar-i-Taiba itself claims to have killed 14,369 Indian soldiers between 1989 and 2000, and to have lost 1,100 *mujahidin*. These groups of *fidayin*, as they are designated within Lashkar-i-Taiba, differ from the suicide squads of the Tamil Tigers or Palestinian Hamas. Islam forbids suicide. There-fore, even if such martyrs are not regarded as having commit-ted suicide, since the Quran declares that they are not dead but live at God's right hand, they nevertheless do not go on mis-sions where death is certain, choosing rather operations where there is a chance, even if it is infinitesimal, of returning alive.

The objective of the *fidayin* is not to martyr themselves in their first operation. On the contrary, they aim to do as much damage as possible to the enemy to inspire fear in both present and future generations. This is why Lashkar-i-Taiba operations against the Hindus are so savage. Women and babies are killed, and victims are beheaded and eviscerated. The ultimate inten-tion is always martyrdom, and families know that *mujahidin* leave their homes with the intention of dying. They return to combat repeatedly until they achieve martyrdom, the most sought-after death. Only a martyr speaks directly to God, and can intercede on behalf of his family and enable its members to enter directly into paradise.[5]

Martyrs are buried in Kashmir, and it is a traditional belief that their bodies remain uncorrupted, and that five or six months after death their flesh is still pink and fresh, and the scent of flowers emanates from their tombs. The district offi-cial of Lashkar-i-Taiba, accompanied by the regional official and a number of *mujahidin*, comes to announce the news to the

[5] For them martyrdom is the sole guarantee of entry to paradise: the observance of the pillars of Islam (the profession of faith, prayer, the pilgrimage, fasting, and the donation of alms) are not sufficient.

family and to offer his congratulations. No display of mourning is allowed for martyrs, since—according to one of the hadiths regularly cited—the Prophet reproached women for lamenting the deaths of their husbands on the field of battle. Instead sweets are distributed, as at a festival. The Lashkar-i-Taiba has devised new rituals to accompany the prayer for the departed (*ghaibana namaz-i-janaza*): the ceremony is most often held on a sports field, and a large crowd assembles; this bestows great prestige on the family and on the village. Visiting senior officials of Lashkar-i-Taiba preside over the ceremonial, transforming it into a politico-religious meeting and, additionally, an opportunity for proselytisation and recruitment. Impassioned orations about *jihad* are delivered, and then the martyr's testament, routinely left with his next of kin, is read in public. This inevitably prompts further volunteers to come forward. The parents of the martyrs are proud to have been singled out to be blessed by God, and are given the chance to express their gratitude at the great annual gatherings of Lashkar-i-Taiba where they speak before tens of thousands of people.

The testaments themselves are usually quite short. All begin with more or less the same phrase: "When you read this testament, I shall have arrived in paradise." The themes covered are always the same. The combatants ask their parents' pardon for leaving them prematurely without having had the time to be of service to them. They also ask the pardon of all those whom they may at any time have harmed, and ask their family to reimburse any modest sums which they may have borrowed from their friends before leaving for Kashmir. They implore the women of their family to observe strict *purdah* (veiling and seclusion), the men to wear their beards, and all to observe scrupulously the five daily prayers. They also ask their families to give a strict religious education to the children, and in addition—this is a recurrent theme—to guard them against the harmful influence of television. They ask their brothers neither to listen to popular songs nor to watch films, and to destroy their television sets and CD players because of the Hindu culture of music, singing and dance which is conveyed through these media.

The family should prevent those who come to pay visits of condolence from weeping, since lamentation for the dead is a grave sin and causes pain to the deceased. The martyrs insist that their brothers must carry forward the banner ("Do not let my Kalashnikov fall") to avenge both their deaths and the humiliations to which the Muslim women of Kashmir have been subjected. All say that they will await their families at the gates of paradise on the day of the Last Judgement, stressing that life in the hereafter is all that counts, life on earth being no more than an ordeal that has to be borne.

The activities of the Lashkar-i-Taiba are not restricted to Kashmir. Its members have also carried out acts of terrorism in India, particularly in the cities of Bombay and Hyderabad. Their aim, which coincides with the interests of the ISI, is to radicalise particular Indian Muslim groups. The *mujahidin* are obliged to promise not to use their arms or their military skills within Pakistan and not to join any ethnic or sectarian group, for example the extremist Deobandi movements.[6] Until the American intervention in Afghanistan, the Lashkar-i-Taiba declared that it had no direct ambitions in Pakistan. Indeed it had no grievance against the Pakistani authorities, and had always enjoyed complete freedom of action within the country in the name of the *jihad* which it waged in Kashmir. However, the centre of Muridke served as an autonomous zone outside the jurisdiction of the state. Ramzi Yusuf[7] and Aimal Kansi[8] among others are said to have taken refuge there.

---

[6] In 1998 Mushahid Hussain, the minister of information in the government of Nawaz Sharif, accompanied the governor of the Punjab to Muridke to enlist the LT's support against sectarian violence.

[7] Yusuf Ramzi was abducted from Pakistan by the US authorities for his part in the World Trade Centre attack in 1993, and imprisoned.

[8] Aimal Kasi killed two CIA employees in Virginia, escaped to Pakistan, and was also abducted at random to the US after a period of liberty, sentenced to death and executed in November 2002. His body was repatriated to Pakistan, where he enjoys martyr status.

The Lashkar-i-Taiba felt itself threatened. It had already been weakened in February 2000 by the Jaish-i-Mohammad's arrival on the scene, or rather its creation by the ISI. It feared, with justice, that it was one of the next targets of American vengeance, and placed little faith in the reassurances of the ISI that it would be permitted to resume its activities in Kashmir once the Afghan crisis was settled. It was for this reason that in October 2001, refusing to follow the instructions of its ISI patrons to keep a low profile, the Lashkar-i-Taiba launched a murderous attack in Kashmir, to match one carried out by the Jaish-i-Mohammad, and afterwards multiplied its attacks on the Indian army and on Hindu civilians. It was probably implicated in the assault on the Indian Parliament on 13 December 2001 which resulted in the deaths of fourteen Indians,—consistently denied by Hafiz Saeed—and in the operation on 14 May 2002 which targeted a garrison near Jammu and left some thirty dead.

Apart from its *jihad* in Kashmir, the Lashkar-i-Taiba may appear as an advocate of "*jihad* for *jihad*'s sake", failing to take the immediate consequences into account. In December 2000 Hafez Saeed declared: "Muslims are organising themselves everywhere in the world to participate in *jihad*.... People demand to know what the *mujahidin* have achieved by waging *jihad* in occupied Kashmir. It is true that we have not yet succeeded in liberating Kashmir, but in my opinion awareness on the part of Muslims of the necessity of *jihad* is much more important than any other outcome." The Lashkar-i-Taiba was banned in January 2002, but in anticipation of this move the armed wing retired to Azad Kashmir and placed itself under an entirely Kashmiri command. It changed its name to Pasban-e Ahl-e hadith and continued its activities. Hafez Saeed became the head of the Jamaat ul-Dawat, based in Muridke, which restricts itself to preaching and education.

The case of the Lashkar-e Taiba is a proof of President Musharraf's ambivalence towards *jihadi* movements. The government has consistently maintained a lenient attitude towards groups focused on the *jihad* in Kashmir because the army will continue to need them as a proxy force for as long as the Kashmir issue remains unsolved. According to the authorities, the Lashkar-e Taiba is 'a real *jihadi* group'—in other words, a group preoccupied only with the *jihad* in Kashmir, which strictly controls its militants, does nothing harmful to the Pakistan government, and is no threat to the country's internal security—consequently the government sees no reason to interfere with its activities.

Hafiz Saeed was released in December 2002 on a court order after spending six months in detention, and immediately started travelling around the country to renew his call for *jihad*. He stresses that *jihad* is essential for the survival of Pakistan and says in interviews that suicide attacks are 'the best form of *jihad*'.

The annual gathering of the movement held in November 2002 in Pattoki attracted over 100,000 people. The magazine *Al Da'wa* has never ceased publication, and its content remains unchanged with a whole section devoted to the testaments of martyrs. Al Da'wa Model schools continue to instill the spirit of *jihad* in children's minds. In 2003 Jamaat ul-Dawat expanded its activities in the areas of health and welfare, notably in Karachi and the interior of Sind.

Other organizations include the Hizb ul-Mujahidin (HM—Party of the Mujahidin), directed by Syed Salahuddin, who came originally from Indian Kashmir and is now resident in Muzaffarabad. Eighty per cent of its recruitment is carried out in Kashmir. More liberal than the Lashkar-i-Taiba and the Jaish-i-Muhammad, it is very close to the Jamaat-i-Islami and demands the annexation of Kashmir to Pakistan. It was the first movement to unleash guerrilla warfare in the mid-1990s, but it declared a unilateral ceasefire in July 2000, which left it relatively marginalised, and led to a major rift inside the movement. Its former chief commander, Abdul Majid Dar, who held talks with the Indian government in Srinagar after this ceasefire, was assassinated in March 2003.

The Tehrik-i-Nifaz-i-Shari'at-i-Muhammadi (TNSM—Movement for the Application of the Shari'a of Muhammad) was founded in 1994 in Malakand by Sufi Muhammad, a dissident member of the Jamaat-i-Islami. It was a tribal party active in the tribal zones and in the North-West Frontier Province, which demanded the application of the Shari'a, and was a typical blend of tribal identity and fundamentalism. In the tradition of Pushtun tribal *jihads* in the nineteenth century, this movement sent at least 7,000 Pushtuns to fight on the side of the Taliban after the start of the American intervention. It was banned in January 2002. More than 5,000 of its members have died in battle or have disappeared in Afghanistan.

Meanwhile, in reaction to the rise of these sectarian movements of Sunni allegiance, the Shi'ites of Pakistan have for their part also organised themselves into political and paramilitary groups. The Sipah-i-Muhammad Pakistan (SMP—Army of Mohammed-Pakistan) was a terrorist group which came out of the Tehrik-i-Jafria-e-Pakistan (TJP—Jafria [Shi'ite] Movement-Pakistan). The TJP was banned in January 2002 and started functioning again under the name of Tehrik-e Islami (TI, Islamic Movement). Its leader Allama Sajid Naqvi is a member of the Muttahida Majlis-e Amal. The SMP was formed in 1994 by Ghulam Raza Naqvi and Murid Abbas Yazdani, who was assassinated in 1996, in reaction to the inability of the TJP to protect the Shi'ites, and its members carried out violent attacks targeted at Sunnis. It recruited in rural areas, in the small villages of southern Punjab and in the Shi'ite *madrasas*. This movement, financed by Iran till 1996 and concentrated in Lahore, was extensively infiltrated by the intelligence services, and fragmented by clashes between personalities and castes. It had an ambiguous relationship with the TJP, on the pattern of that between the Sipah-i-Sabaha-Pakistan with the Lashkar-i-Jangvi. Since 1998, the Sipah-i-Muhammad-Pakistan has virtually disintegrated, with its militants either in prison or in exile in Iran and southern Lebanon. What remains is a collection of uncontrolled and extremely violent elements without a unified structure of command, who carry out reprisals for anti-Shi'ite attacks. The Sipah-i-Mohammad was banned in August 2001.

5. Connections and Dynamics

Although in the 1990s ex-Soviet Central Asia, Afghanistan and Pakistan were the scene of a spectacular multiplication of Islamic movements, these were not centrally coordinated. Personal rivalries, ethnic divisions between Uzbeks, Tajiks, Pushtuns, Punjabis and Sindhis, and caste divisions in Pakistan, in addition to differing strategies, often placed such movements in opposition to each other, or at least obstructed any real unity between them. However, networks of personal relationships often played a substantial role, especially among the former Islamic volunteers who fought in Afghanistan from 1984 to 1992, and in the context of relationships between masters and pupils or among contemporaries in the Pakistani *madrasas*, all based on ethnic connections.

The Central Asian movements are not coordinated among themselves, even if relationships between commanders do exist on the ground. Uzbeks and Tajiks fought shoulder to shoulder between 1992 and 1997, with the consequence that members of the Islamic Movement of Uzbekistan were able to find refuge and protection in the upper Gharm valley in Tajikistan between 1998 and 2000. The Taliban did not play a coordinating role; they were part of the general military agglomeration, but were not at its centre. Their particular function was to give refuge to fleeing militants and lay the groundwork for the construction of Islamic fighting formations in which ethnic origins would supposedly no longer be an issue. Afghanistan served as a melting-pot for a new generation of transnational combatants, but it was not the headquarters of radical Islamism.

The two truly international conglomerations were the Bin Laden network (al-Qaida) and the Pakistani movements. They took parallel paths and remained institutionally distinct, eventhough they displayed affinity after the Gulf War of 1991.

The al-Qaida movement and the Afghans

The radicalisation of al-Qaida was to be fully realised from the time that Bin Laden returned to Afghanistan from Sudan and assumed direct control. Between 1992, when Kabul fell into the hands of Massoud, and 1996, when it was taken by the Taliban, the foreign volunteers present in Afghanistan did not appear to be centralised and lacked clear objectives. Some fought on the side of Hekmatyar against Massoud, but the majority were attached to local commanders, who were nearly all Pushtuns. For example, in the Pushtun pocket around Kunduz in the north, there was a strong Arab presence attached to the Saudi-based International Islamic Relief Organisation; the latter concerned itself particularly with the Tajik refugee camps, which it barred Westerners from entering. Similarly, in the Kunar valley close to the Pakistani frontier, small Afghan emirates were set up which were practically the counterparts of the Pakistani Islamist movement Dawat wal Irshad, led by Muhammad Afzal in Upper Nuristan and Jamil al-Rahman among the Safi tribe of Pesh, also in that region. In 1992 Massoud's administration in Kabul had no Arab member, and he was not unduly concerned by the presence of Arabs on Afghan soil. There were regular clashes between the Afghan population and the Arabs, who for want of clear aims took to making periodical denunciations of what they regarded as popular superstitions, such as visits to the tombs of saints and the displaying of flags at the tombs of martyrs.

The encounter between Bin Laden and the Taliban changed the rules. The Taliban entrusted to Bin Laden control of the non-Pakistani militants, while the Pakistani organisations, especially the Harakat ul-Mujahidin, took control of a number of training camps in the province of Paktia. In 1996 the Harakat ul-Ansar were given the task of managing the Salman ul-Farsi training camp in Paktia after the Hizb ul-Mujahidin militants, connected to Hekmatyar, were driven out by the Taliban. The camp was re-named Amir Muawiya (founder of the Umayyad dynasty in the Seventh century CE) and became a sanctuary for the anti-Shi'ite militants of the Lashkar-i-Jhangvi. The Al-Badr 1 and 2 camps of the Jamaat-i-Islami were also given to Harakat ul-Ansar.

During this period Bin Laden brought the Arabs under his control and isolated them from the Afghan population. The leaders were installed in what amounted to residential complexes near Kandahar and Jalalabad, while the ordinary fighters were grouped together in cantonments in Kabul and Kunduz. At the same time a third echelon was established, made up of militants from Western countries who were being trained to return home and carry out terrorist activities. A select group functioned in Afghanistan under the leadership of Abu Zubayda; this Palestinian from Gaza, born in the Saudi capital Riyadh in 1971 and holding an Egyptian passport, was a former member of Islamic Jihad and resident in Afghanistan.

The leaders came almost entirely from the first generation of militants who had come to Afghanistan to fight the Russians, with the exception of Bin Laden's spokesman, a Kuwaiti named Suleiman Abu Gheith who became a close aide of Bin Laden, and was seen sitting beside him in the post-September 11 videos. This group included Bin Laden, Ayman al-Zawahiri and Mohammed Atef, *alias* Abdulaziz Abu Sitta, *alias* Tasir Abdullah, *alias* Abu Hafs al-Misri—a former Egyptian police officer who had been in Peshawar since 1983 and whose daughter had married Bin Laden's son.

However, a new generation of Bin Laden's militants arrived, who differed from the veterans of the 1980s. In general these new arrivals did not come directly from the Middle East, and were not distinguished for their political insight or for any pre-existing religious commitment. Whatever their nationality, whether they were from Arab countries or from the West, they had been re-Islamised in the West, often through contact with Arab "Afghans" (i.e. veterans of the fighting in Afghanistan) who were attached to the radical mosques. One of the best known of these mosques is the one at Finsbury Park in London, directed by Abu Hamza, an Egyptian political refugee in London since 1981, who had served his time in Afghanistan. Zacarias Moussaoui, Djamel Beghal, Kamel Daoudi and Ahmed Ressam, all of whom are on trial at the time of writing for involvement in the al-Qaida network, passed through this mosque enroute to Afghanistan.

The perpetrators of the attacks of 11 September 2001, or at least the leaders of the group, had similar profiles. They were educated and well assimilated in the West, where they were studying, and had left their family circles and emigrated from their countries of origin. They were the "second generation" of Muslims, who threw themselves abruptly into radicalisation without passing through the intermediate stages of religious or political militancy. Although their origins were similar to those of the first generation—they come from the Gulf countries, Algeria and Egypt—their profile was different in the sense that they routinely came by way of a period spent in the West and by way of a phase of activism, without a previous one of piety and religious observance (Bin Laden had studied religion, and then become progressively radicalised over a long period). Within this category were the two assassins of Massoud, one of whom, Dahman Abd al-Fattah, was a Tunisian graduate in journalism who had attended three universities in Belgium. Another noteworthy case among the "Afghans" was Abdelilah Zyad, a Moroccan resident in France, who was sentenced to eight years in prison for the Marrakesh incident of 24 August 1994.[1] To this second generation should be added, finally, a third category—that of the converts, who had not existed in the 1980s except for Black Americans.

---

[1] Youths of Algerian and Moroccan origin settled in France murdered Spanish tourists in the reception area of a hotel in Marrakesh.

The relationship between members of this second generation and Afghanistan was also different. They never mixed with the Afghan population, living apart with volunteers from other countries. They were hardly interested in their local surroundings and came to Afghanistan only to be trained there to take part in the global *jihad* against the United States, in which neo-fundamentalism and classic anti-imperialism were mingled. As rebellious youths, disaffected from their societies, they became the tools of al-Qaida. They fought bravely, as their resistance to the joint attacks of the Americans and the Northern Alliance in 2001 proved, but their separation from the population and their ignorance of the language and of local society made them vulnerable and unfit for guerrilla warfare. However, their methods of combat, which were completely distinct from the Afghan tradition and included the suicide attack on Massoud on 9 September and the uprising of the prisoners of Qala-i-Jangi on 25 November 2001, demonstrated that they could overturn the traditional order.

A final significant element was that within the framework of al-Qaida militants from different countries would find themselves operating side by side. Could this solidarity survive the disappearance of the organisation as such? There exists at least one example: the link between the brother of Yusuf Ramzi (Wali Khan) and the brother of Janjalani, who went together to the Philippines where they attempted to mount an attack on the Pope in December 1995.

In every case the leadership of al-Qaida proves to be international, with a strong Arab representation. In 1998 Bin Laden announced the creation of an international Islamic Front for *jihad* against the "Crusaders" and the Jews. This front included the Pakistani Lashkar-i-Taiba, the Egyptian Jihad and Gamaat, the Pakistani Harakat ul-Mujahidin, and militants of other national origins. The dominant components were nevertheless Pakistani and Egyptian. The Majlis al-Shura, the movement's consultative council, comprised—in addition to Bin Laden himself—Zawahiri, Zubayda and Atta, who were Egyptian, and the Uzbeks Yoldashev and Namangani (according to the partial information which it has been possible to obtain).

The fusion between the Taliban and al-Qaida. In the light of the chronology of events, it could have appeared that the Taliban movement became radicalised under the pressure of events but that it did not share the jihadist ideology of Osama Bin Laden. However, after the military campaign of October and November 2001 new factors indicated the extent to which the aims of al-Qaida and those of the Taliban had come together. This process of convergence probably dates from the year 2000, when from the autumn onwards manifestations of radicalisation began to appear. These included the eradication of the opium poppy, which served only to undermine the Taliban's support in the society of the region. Another instance was the destruction of the statues of Buddha at Bamiyan, which had existed throughout the entire Islamic period; this was carried out in the teeth of Pakistani pressure and the unanimous advice of the Arab *ulema*. Further factors were the obligation on Hindus and Sikhs resident in Kabul to wear distinctive symbols, and the arrest of Christian aid workers on charges of proselytisation. Finally, the declaration by Mullah Omar to the BBC on 15 November 2001 calling for the destruction of America indicated his ideological alignment with Bin Laden.

Without the role played by al-Qaida, the Taliban, who have never been accused of playing an active part in the attacks of 11 September, would in all probability have continued in power. It is a paradox that foreign influence brought about the fall of the Taliban. By accentuating the ideological aspect of the Taliban phenomenon, al-Qaida severed its linkage with traditional Afghan society. The political agenda was in fact dictated by Osama Bin Laden, but the local dynamics in the end tilted the balance in favour of the American intervention. It is certainly the case that the foreigners were only a reinforcement and not a decisive strategic element in the regional context, even though al-Qaida succeeded in taking control of the Taliban, or at least of Mullah Omar's immediate circle.

The role of Pakistan

In Pakistan two concurrent phenomena have played a determining role in the evolution of the Islamic movements since the first Afghan war. These are the strategy of the Pakistani army and hence *a fortiori* of the military intelligence service (ISI); and the radicalisation of the traditional movements.

The Pakistani military intelligence services and the radical tendency. The Pakistani military intelligence services have always made use of, and supported, the Islamic radical movements in the context of the regional policy of Pakistan in Afghanistan and Kashmir. This relationship was not only a matter of tactical exploitation. Some senior officials of the ISI became increasingly close to the Islamic radicals. These included Hamid Gul and Osman Khalid, as became clear from the positions they adopted after their retirement. However, religious convictions do not in themselves explain the relationship, which was essentially the result of a carefully thought-out regional policy that the Pakistani army and the ISI supported the Islamists, especially after General Zia ul-Haq seized power in 1977. During the Afghan war the principal beneficiary of their aid was Hekmatyar's Hizb-i-Islami. Subsequently it was the Taliban.

There were clear links between the ISI and certain extremist movements active on the domestic front and in Kashmir. It was with the aid of the ISI that Dawat wal Irshad created Lashkar-i-Taiba (the Army of the Pure) in 1990. The ISI changed its tactics in Kashmir in 1993 following the attack on a group of Western tourists at Srinagar in 1992; from this date onwards the Pakistani secret services no longer operated openly in Kashmir but cloaked their activities behind intermediaries in what amounted to nothing less than a sub-contracting and privatisation of the *jihad*. They also halted financial support for movements aimed at the independence of Kashmir and only helped those that favoured its annexation to Pakistan. This meant that the Jammu and Kashmir Liberation Front lost much of its influence to the advantage of the Hizb ul-Mujahidin, who was active on the ground and linked to Jamaat-i-Islami. This faction in its turn was supplanted by more radical movements at the instigation of the Pakistani authorities. Indeed, after the destruction of the Babri mosque at Ayodhya in December 1992 the Pakistani secret services also aimed to profit from the radicalisation of Indian Muslims by recruiting motivated youths and training them, in Kashmir among other places, so that they would be able to attack Hindus throughout India. Finally, the ISI wanted movements active in Kashmir to attack the Hindus of Jammu and the Buddhists of Ladakh and so frighten them into leaving Kashmir. The Hizb ul-Mujahidin was reluctant to do this, since it wished to restrict its operations to Kashmir, but other movements, such as the Harakat ul-Mujahidin and the Lashkar-i-Taiba, were prepared to extend their activities beyond Kashmir and therefore became, after 1994, the groups favoured by the ISI. General Pervez Musharraf, then chief of staff, called on the Lashkar-i-Taiba to reinforce his offensive in Kashmir in the spring of 1999 in the Kargil sector.[2]

A kind of escalation took place. For complex reasons the Pakistani secret services encourage splits in the radical movements. This was partly to be able to control them better, but was also in order to cover the tracks left by their operations. The Jaish-i-Mohammad was apparently set up with ISI support as a counterweight to the Lashkar-i-Taiba, which had become too powerful in Kashmir. This was a relative setback, since far from reining in the tempo of terrorist action it caused

---

[2] For further details see J.-L. Racine, *Cachemire. Au péril de la guerre*, Paris: Autrement, 2002.

the two movements to compete so that each would seek to carry out more spectacular operations than the other.[3] An additional reason for the ISI's encouragement of splits is its desire to separate the Afghan and Kashmiri *jihads* and to distance the Pushtuns from operations in Kashmir. The intention behind the establishment of the Jaish-i-Mohammad was to give a Kashmiri and Punjabi face to the *jihad*, and to localise the training camps in Kashmir.

The sacking of General Mahmud Ahmed, director of the ISI, after the 11 September attack because of his Islamist orientation was also precipitated by the attack on 1 October 2001 against the regional assembly in Srinagar, an especially symbolic target, in which thirty people were killed. Responsibility for this attack was claimed by the Jaish-i-Muhammad, and although this was almost immediately repudiated, India launched a campaign against Pakistan, which it accused of supporting the movement. The Jaish-i-Muhammad normally avoided contact with the press, but some individual members had contacted newspapers to claim responsibility for the attack. The question naturally arises: who asked them to do this, and why? No doubt it needed to be proved that official Pakistani approval of the American intervention in Pakistan did not mean a slackening of the country's interest in Kashmir.

The ISI also supported the Taliban at the time of their rise to power in 1994. General Naseerullah Babar, Pakistan's Minister of the Interior, paid a visit to the Taliban in October 1994, and Colonel Imam, its consul-general in Herat,[4] helped them to take that city in 1995. A pro-Taliban lobby thus came into being in Pakistan, run both by retired officers, including Hamid Gul and Aslam Beg, and by Deobandi circles, including Fazlur Rehman and Sami ul-Haq. At that time General Hamid Gul, as Defence Attaché at the Pakistani embassy in Kabul,

---

[3] Cf. the responsibility claimed by the two movements for attacks after 11 September.

[4] A post he had held since 1994 and still occupied in 2001.

supervised the training of commandos. A number of senior officers were seconded to the Taliban, and in 2000 these were General Said Safar and General Irshad—who was wounded and replaced by General Munir. In November 2001 the Pakistanis had to send several aircraft to rescue their officers who became trapped in Kunduz with the besieged Taliban and al-Qaida militants during the Northern Alliance offensive. Sipah-i-Sahaba militias participated directly in the fighting against Massoud, and were probably responsible for the murder of Iranian diplomats at Mazar-i-Sherif in the north of Afghanistan in August 1998. Two other groups which took part were the Harakat ul-Mujahidin and the Jaish-i-Muhammad, whose base was at Rishkor, south of Kabul.

This pro-Taliban policy certainly put Islamabad in direct contact with the activist Islamic networks. However, to avoid an overt clash with Washington, it has always handed over to the Americans activists who were explicitly identified as the perpetrators of terrorist actions. Aimal Kasi (who carried out an attack on CIA operatives at Langley, Virginia, in January 1993), Yusuf Ramzi (a nephew of Khalid Sheikh Muhammad and master-mind of the attack on the World Trade Center in February 1993) and Mohammed Sadiq Odeh (behind the attack on the US embassies in Nairobi and Dar es Salaam in August 1998) were arrested and extradited to the United States between 1994 and 1996, despite violent objections from General Hamid Gul. In addition, no suspect would ever be handed over without a specific request being made by the Americans.

The attack of 11 September 2001 certainly changed the situation. Washington then did what it had previously refused to do, namely exert strong pressure on Pakistan to sever its links with the Taliban and with Bin Laden's radicals. Hence, after the American bombing of Afghanistan in August 1998, the ISI found itself in a delicate position: it made a great effort, more or less successfully, to give the impression that the Afghan and Kashmiri *jihads* had been isolated from each other, especially by creating splits within the radical movements. The Pakistani military intelligence services still hoped for American support over Kashmir, even while they were arming and supporting anti-American, anti-Israeli and anti-Saudi groups with the sole intention of destabilising India. However, these groups were definitively declared by the United States to be terrorists, or had their sources of finance placed under close surveillance. After 11 September 2001 Britain put the Lashkar-i-Taiba on the list of prohibited terrorist movements, and this gave rise to a vicious campaign by Hafiz Saeed against Western culture and particularly against the Christian schools in Pakistan.

However, Washington clearly distinguished between Kashmir and Afghanistan, with the effect that Pakistani activist groups, even while they were being placed on terrorist registers, were not subjected to real repression and kept their capacity for militant action intact.

Pakistani Islamists at the heart of transnational links

The radicalisation of the conservative Islamic movements took place in the wake of the incident caused by the publication of Salman Rushdie's novel *The Satanic Verses* in 1988, and more especially after the Gulf War. It reached its peak with the American bombing campaign against the Taliban in 1998. The traditionalist movements at that time became explicitly anti-American and began to advocate *jihad*. This radicalisation took place alongside the growing use by the Pakistani army of its Islamic auxiliaries. Bin Laden became a popular hero, and two mass gatherings in Pakistan, with the participation of the retired generals, mobilised the Islamist tendency in Pakistan against the United States.

A breakdown of the foreign prisoners held by Massoud[5] shows that 39 per cent belonged to the Pakistani Harakat ul-Mujahidin movement (*alias* Harakat ul-Ansar). Only thirty-

[5] Julie Stirrs (formerly of the Intelligence and Research Department of the US State Department), "The Taliban's International Ambitions", *Middle East Quarterly*, summer 2001.

three out of 110 Pakistanis identified themselves as Pushtuns, which indicates that the basis of Pakistani support went well beyond ethnic solidarity. Even more oddly, the other political affiliations were extremely varied. Members of Jamaat al-Tabligh were present, but so too were adherents of Nawaz Sharif's Muslim League, demonstrating that radicalisation had in fact penetrated to militants of all backgrounds, including political parties which rejected armed struggle. Only 43 per cent of the 110 were students of religion. The foreign presence in the Pakistani madrasas was less measurable and seemed to be proportionally less significant. In March 2002, the authorities counted 35,000 foreign students, of whom 16,000 were Afghans and 15,000 Arabs. It is certain that networks interpenetrate. Young Pakistanis living in Britain and captured in Afghanistan had often spent time in the Pakistani *madrasas*.

The transnational links between the Pakistani Islamists and the Taliban and al-Qaida do not appear to have an organisational base. In reality everything rests on personal connections, the connections of the *madrasas*, chance meetings in training camps and community of interest. An example of this fluidity is the case of Sheikh Omar Saeed, who was liberated along with Masood Azhar at the time of the hijacking of the Indian Airlines plane in December 1999 and was afterwards with the Taliban and Bin Laden in Kandahar. A British citizen, born in 1973 into a wealthy Pakistani family in the textile business in London, he moved to Lahore and was imprisoned in India for the kidnapping of three Western tourists in Kashmir, an operation he organised in order to bring about Masood Azhar's release. He had been educated at Aitchison School at Lahore for two years, and afterwards studied at the London School of Economics. Then in 1993 he went to Bosnia on a humanitarian mission, where he came in contact with Pakistani militants belonging to Harakat ul Ansar. A few months later he was back in Pakistan where he underwent training in Miranshah (Waziristan) and then in the Khalid bin Waleed camp in Afghanistan, where he became an instructor, and where he reportedly met Masood Azhar who asked him to go to India. Sheikh Omar returned to Britain in 1994 and obtained an Indian visa on his British passport. After a short stay in the Harakat ul Ansar training camp near Jalalabad in Afghanistan, he was sent to India with the mission to capture Westerners in exchange for Masood Azhar. He is said to have transferred US$ 100,000 from Pakistan via Dubai to Muhammad Atta, one of the perpetrators of the 11 September attack. He is also said to have been linked to the Pakistani intelligence services, and in particular to Mahmud Ahmed, who was dismissed as ISI director by General Musharraf, and is also supposed to have been an agent for al-Qaida in Lahore. Unlike Masood Azhar, he kept a low profile after his release and allegedly shuttled between Pakistan and Afghanistan. He apparently had connections with Abu Zubaida and with Ramzi Binalshibh and Khalid Sheikh Mohammad. In February 2002 he was arrested for the abduction of the *Wall Street Journal* journalist Daniel Pearl, who was murdered by his kidnappers. On 5 February Sheikh Omar Saeed is known to have gone to the house of Ejaz Shah, the provincial Minister of the Interior and a former official of the ISI. His arrest was announced on 12 February, at the end of a visit to the United States by General Musharraf. Sheikh Omar Saeed was sentenced to death on 15 July 2002 for his involvement in the kidnapping and murder of Daniel Pearl, and at the time of going to press his appeal is pending before the High Court. Although the United States asked for his extradition, President Musharraf has reiterated that as 'a principled stand' he would not extradite him or any Pakistani national suspected of helping the Taliban or Al Qaida networks.

Another notable personality is Mufti Nizamuddin Shamzai, the spritual adviser of Mullah Omar, principal of the *madrasa* at Binori Town in Karachi and the teacher of Masood Azhar. He supported the Jaish-i-Mohammad in whose establishment he participated, was a member of the Zia ul-Haq's Majlis-i-Shura, and belonged to the Jami'at-i-Ulema-Islam. He travelled to South Africa, among other destinations, to persuade Muslim communities to support the Taliban, and in early October 2001 was a member of the delegation which went to Kandahar with General Mahmud Ahmed, officially to persuade Mullah Omar to abandon Bin Laden but in fact to encourage the Mullah not to give in. Mufti Shamzai, who was present at the marriage of Osama Bin Laden's eldest son in 2000, issued a *fatwa* in September 2001 calling on Muslims to wage jihad against the United States if they attacked Afghanistan. The *fatwa* also stated that according to the Shari'a citizens of Muslim countries which supported the United States or any other infidel force were no longer obliged to obey their governments. Mufti Shamzai developed a method of recruiting volunteers which ensured that no-one could be signed up without careful screening.

A third example of the Islamic connection between Taliban Afghanistan, al-Qaida and Pakistan was the link between Abdullah Azzam, Osama Bin Laden and the Markaz Dawat wal Irshad, to whose establishment Bin Laden appears to have made a significant financial contribution. It should be remembered that Osama Bin Laden regularly spoke to the annual conventions of Lashkar-i-Taiba by telephone, from Sudan in 1995 and 1996 and from Afghanistan in 1997. The Markaz Dawat wal Irshad, which had been close to Saudi Arabia during the Gulf War, had afterwards distanced itself from the kingdom for the same reasons as Osama Bin Laden had done so. These were the stationing of American troops on Saudi soil, and allegations of corruption against Saudi society and the Saudi royal family. After the model of Harakat ul-Mujahidin, the Lashkar-i-Taiba became part of the International Islamic Front for Jihad, created by Bin Laden in 1998, in opposition to the United States and Israel. This move gave concern to the Pakistani authorities.

The Pakistani Islamists in general expressed their support for the Taliban through mass meetings. For instance, a meeting was organised by Sami ul-Haq on 10 January 2001 at Akora

Khattak to protest against the adoption of UN Security Council resolution 1333 against the Taliban. This brought together the Jami'at-i-Ulema of Pakistan (JUP), from the more moderate wing; the Jamaat-i-Islami, through its leader Qazi Hussein Ahmed; the Jami'at-Ulema-i-Islam, also through its leader Maulana Fazlur Rehman; the Sipah-i-Sahaba with Maulana Azam Tariq; the leader of the Jami'at-i-Ahl-i-Hadith, Moheenuddin Lakhvi; the head of the Ikhwan, Muhammad Akram Awan; the head of the Tehrik-i-Islami, Dr Israr Muhammad; Maulana Sufi Muhammad of the Tehrik-i-Nifaz-i-Shari'at-i-Muhammadi; General Hamid Gul; General Aslam Beg; Ejaz ul-Haq, son of General Zia ul-Haq; Mufti Nizamuddin Shamzai; Maulana Masood Azhar of the Jaish-i-Muhammad; the head of the Harakat ul-Jihad, Muhammad Saeed; the head of the Harakat ul-Mujahidin, Fazlur Rehman Khalil; Bakhat Zamin of the al-Badr Mujahidin; and the leader of the Jami'at ul-Mujahidin, Mufti Bashir Ahmed Kashmiri.

Following the announcement of the American campaign in 2001, the majority of these movements joined the Pak-Afghan Defence Council, founded in December 2000 by Maulana Sami ul-Haq in protest at the UN-supported international sanctions against the Taliban but there was no agreement on strategy. Shamzai and Fazlur Rehman wanted a confrontation with the Musharraf government, while factions like the Jami'at-i-Ulema-Pakistan were more cautions. Nevertheless at the moment of the anti-American demonstrations in the autumn of 2001, the protest movement against the American campaign took on a purely Pushtun ethnic aspect. Even in Karachi at least 80 per cent of the demonstrators were Pushtuns. The same applied to the Pakistani volunteers captured in Afghanistan during the campaign of 2001, in contrast to the variety among those taken prisoner earlier. These were Pusthuns, even though the Northern Alliance characterised them as "Punjabis". This ethnic connection explains why the demonstrations were concentrated in Peshawar, Quetta and Karachi, and did not touch Lahore and Rawalpindi.

Here one can observe the structural limitations of the Pakistani religious movements. Behind a façade of unanimity and the radicalisation of their language in favour of the Shari'a and against the Americans and Musharraf, they were deeply divided along ethnic and caste lines. Support for the Taliban has been above all based on the Pushtun connection, which explains the role played by the small-scale movement of Maulana Sufi Muhammad, the Tehrik-i-Nifaz-i-Shari'a-i-Muhammadi (TSNM), which is based in tribal Pushtun areas. However, the Baluchis, the Sindhis and the Muhajirs, who are in any case less susceptible to the prevalent neo-fundamentalism, have remained aloof from mobilisation, while the Punjabis will only act if Musharraf gives up Kashmir, which the Americans have not asked him to do.

The Pakistanisation of Al Qaida

After the fall of the Taliban, the militants, including those who had returned from Afghanistan, regrouped in Karachi with the support of some elements of the ISI, which had not been entirely purged. The militants were disillusioned with their leaders, who had not been able to unite against the government to prevent it from allying itself with the United States. Keen to show that their capacity to cause trouble was undiminished, they mounted spectacular operations against targets hitherto spared, including Westerners and women. This magnified the repercussions of their actions and further weakened Musharraf, who became a hostage to these movements, and was now perceived as incapable of defending either Pakistani citizens or foreigners. These operations, all carried out after 12 January, included the kidnapping of Daniel Pearl on 23 January 2002; the assassination of Shi'ite doctors in Karachi; the attack in March 2002 on the Protestant church in the diplomatic quarter of Islamabad which caused the deaths of five people, including two Americans; the attack deliberately aimed at Shi'ite women and children in a place of worship at Bhakkar in April; the attack in Karachi on 8 May which caused the deaths of eleven employees at the French Naval Construction Department at Cherbourg as well as three Pakistanis; the attack on the American consulate in Karachi on 14 June which caused twelve deaths; the attack on a missionary school in Murree on 5 August which killed six; and the attack on a missionary hospital in Taxila on 9 August which killed four. Musharraf evidently understood the message because, following the kidnapping and killing of Daniel Pearl, repression of the jihadists halted until attacks on Westerners began in earnest. Meanwhile the Pakistani secret services did nothing to hinder the regrouping of the Pakistani and Arab jihadists within Pakistan.

From May 2002 the government started blaming every act of terrorism on the Lashkar-e Jhangvi, which was described by the authorities as the Pakistani wing of Al Qaida. Putting the blame on Lashkar-e Jhangvi had a dual purpose: it showed the United States that Pakistan was really cooperating in the war against Al Qaida, while at the same time showing Pakistani public opinion that the government was serious in dealing with sectarian terrorism.

After the attacks on Westerners in 2002 the police arrested many activists, who were invariably described as belonging to the Lashkar-e Jhangvi. This raised a number of questions. To attribute responsibility for every terrorist act to a peripheral sectarian outfit which had been banned before September 11 seemed a very convenient way to protect the real perpetrators of the attacks and movements such as the Harakat al Jihad al Islami (HUJI) or the Harakat al Mujahidin al Alami (HUMA), especially because those arrested were never brought to trial but instead eliminated in false encounters. This modus operandi enabled the authorities to avoid bringing sensitive cases to trial and prevented the prisoners of making incriminating statements which would have put in doubt their alleged affiliation with al Qaida. On the other hand, it seems that the police had succeeded in infiltrating the Lashkar-e Jhangvi and to some extent dismantling it. This was confirmed by the arrest of its main activists in the following months, including Akram

Lahori (whose real name is Muhammad Ajmal), who had been involved in thirty-eight cases of sectarian terrorism. This former bodyguard of Haq Nawaz Jhangvi, founder of the SSP, who had been active in terrorist activities since 1990, was arrested in June 2002. Ghulam Shabbir (alias Shabbir Fauji), who had trained the militants in Afghanistan for several years, was arrested in October 2002. The arrest of Qari Asadullah (alias Qari Abdul Hay, or Talha), chief of a breakaway faction of the Lashkar-e Jhangvi, was officially announced in May 2003. Described as the 'mastermind' of Pearl's murder, he had left Pakistan in 1997 to become the trainer at the Sarobi camp in Afghanistan. He was said to be an expert in explosives and chemicals, and had returned to Pakistan after the fall of the Taliban. His group enjoyed support in Karachi while Basra and his followers had a strong following in Punjab. As with most extremist outfits in Pakistan, ideology was never really a factor in the splits within the Lashkar-e Jhangvi, personality clashes among the leaders being the main cause.

The death of Asif Ramzi in December 2002 was a severe blow to the group. This member of the Gujarati Memon community, who belonged to Qari Asadullah's faction and claimed to have created the Muslim Unified Army (MUA), was the link with the Arabs who provided funds at a time when Lashkar-e Jhangvi was short of money. The official version of how he met his death was that he had been killed by the wrongly-timed explosion of a bomb, but he may have been eliminated by the agencies or by fellow activists. Nadeem Abbas, a member of the SSP and constable in the Sindh Anti-Corruption Establishment, was also killed in the blast.

Al Qaida militants who had initially found a safe haven in the tribal areas and later moved to Azad Kashmir, Punjab and Karachi would not have been able to do so without the connivance of the ISI. The authorities have confirmed that the militants who killed ten Pakistani soldiers and paramilitaries in Waziristan on 25 June 2002 were Uzbeks belonging to the IMU. In addition, several hundred members of Al-Qaida are said to have reached Azad Kashmir with the assistance of the Lashkar-i-Taiba among others. According to Pakistani intelligence agencies, at the beginning of 2003 between 200 and 300 Al Qaida activists were hiding in Pakistan.

There seems to be disillusionment among Al Qaida activists with the Pushtuns whom they often suspect of giving information to American intelligence officers. Actually they rely on the strong support networks which they have built among Pakistani Islamic parties during the Afghan war in the 1980s. Members of these groups give them shelter in the cities of Punjab and in Karachi, where they often hide in upmarket areas.

So, even if weakened, Al Qaida is very much alive in Pakistan and particularly in Karachi where *jihad* has been centralized, and which has become its new hub. It has been relatively easy for activists to merge into the population of Karachi, a megapolis of 15 million inhabitants where law enforcement is weak, where the ISI has kept its networks and which the security services do not control effectively—all the more so since as some of their operatives share the ideology of the activists. There have been several instances when Al Qaida suspects escaped just before the American raids in Pakistan, apparently having been tipped off.

As Al Qaida militants have fled to Pakistan, so have the local *jihadi* groups increasingly cooperated with them. The level of coordination and of organisation of the attacks launched in Pakistan from the spring of 2002 and the new methods including suicide bombings clearly point to Al Qaida being implicated. Groups which were active in Kashmir (like Jaish-e Muhammad) or whose sole aim was to kill Shiites (like the Laskhar-e Jhangvi) have merged operationally and started participating in anti-Western operations. However, the West is not the only target: in the message of Osama Bin Laden broadcast by Al Jazira on 11 February 2003, Pakistan was included in the list of so-called anti-Muslim apostate states (like Nigeria and Morocco) enslaved by the United States which have to be liberated through *jihad*.

The links between the Pakistani movements and Al Qaida were exposed to the light of day at the time of the arrest of Abu Zubayda, who had been in the forefront of reorganizing Al Qaida in Pakistan, on 28 March 2002 in Faisalabad, the field of the radical Deobandi movements, and of some fifty Al-Qaida members, including twenty Arabs who were transferred to the US detention camp at Guantanamo Bay in Cuba. This arrest clearly put the spotlight on the links between the Lashkar-e Taiba and Arab militants—Abu Zubayda had been given shelter by local Lashkar-e Taiba office-holders. Two other top Al Qaida leaders were arrested: Ramzi Binalshibh, a Yemeni national member of the Hamburg cell, on 11 September 2002 in Karachi, and Khalid Sheikh Mohammad, a Pakistani born in Kuwait, on 1 March 2003 in Rawalpindi. This was only a few days after the arrest in Quetta of Mohammad Abdul Rehman, son of Umar Abdul Rehman, the blind Egyptian religious leader now in prison in the United States. The links between the Arabs and Lashkar-e Taiba came to light once again after the arrest on 29 April 2003 in Karachi of Ali Abd al Aziz (also known as Ammar al Baluchi), another nephew of Khalid Sheikh Muhammad who reportedly financed the September 11 hijackers, and of Waleed Muhammad bin Attash, a Yemeni suspected of the attack on the USS *Cole* at Aden in October 2000. This man is reported to have stated that he was recruiting Pakistani volunteers for suicide missions against American targets and already had a dozen recruits from the Lashkar-e Taiba. Large quantities of explosives and weapons have been seized in Karachi. The Jaish-e Muhammad is also believed by many observers to be part of the al-Qaida network and to have sent fighters to aid the Iraqi resistance against the United States.

In the absence of a centralized direction, makeshift alliances made of small groups decentralized and split into extremely compartimentalized cells of two or three members are operating with increasing autonomy against targets of opportunity identified with the United States. They have in common the fact that their members have been in training camps in Afghanistan.

They keep changing their names, and those they adopt—such as the Muslim United Army (MUA), Hizbullah al Alami, and Harakat ul Mujahidin ul Alami (HUMA)—tend to emphasise their transnational nature by using the terms *alami* (international) or united.

Asif Zaheer, who was arrested in December 2002 and sentenced to death for his involvement in the suicide-bomb attack against the French engineers in May 2002, was making bombs for different *jihadi* groups. He had been trained in Afghanistan and returned to Pakistan before the fall of the Taliban. He was heading his own faction of the Harkat ul Jihad ul Islami (HUJI), and formed Harkat al Mujahidin al Alami (HUMA). The Muslim United Army, which claims to be an alliance of *jihadi* groups (notably the Lashkar-e Jhangvi and the Harakat ul Mujahidin) and whose logo is a sword piercing the globe, came out in October 2002 when it claimed responsibility for a series of parcel-bomb attacks in Karachi targeting police officials. In an email message Asif Ramzi, chief of his own faction of the Lashkar-e Jhangvi, wrote: 'All the rightwing organisations have formed the Muslim United Army to organise groups against the United States. We are going to launch a war against anti-Islamic forces, police and other non-Muslims on the platform of the MUA.' Pakistani police did not take it seriously till 15 May 2003 when twenty-one petrol stations owned by Shell in Karachi were attacked with small bombs. The MUA claimed responsibility for the explosions and warned that major attacks would follow if the government did not stop its operations against *mujahidin*.

The blurring of strategic and ideological alignments

The new radical Islamic tendency blurs the ideological and strategic lines of division which were so clearly laid down in the 1980s. Iran has the same enemy as the United States: the Taliban. The Pakistani army furthers the cause of the radical Islamists. The Taliban, which is a conservative and anti-

communist movement, is radicalised against the Americans
and finds an echo of sympathy within the Saudi ideological
structure, dominated by Wahhabi *ulema* who are nevertheless
in an alliance with the Americans. The Russians simultaneously
fight the Islamists and make use of them, for example at the
time of the aerial evacuation of Islamists trapped in Kyrgyzstan
in the autumn of 2000. At a time when the struggle against
Bin Laden's networks has increasingly taken on the nature of
a security and police operation, the Islamic radicalisation of
Pakistan, a state possessing nuclear capability, poses yet more
difficult problems.

A new relationship exists between interests of state, viewed
independently of ideological issues, and transnational networks
of a kind which may operate even within the heartland of
countries officially allied to the United States. However, the
existence of these transnational networks does not itself constitute a novel strategic threat, since their operations are always
conceived in the context of local considerations. The networks
operate with two sets of criteria in view, the local and the
global. One should not allow the resemblances between the
language in which the two are set forth, with their appeal to
the *jihad* and the *umma*, to hide the essentially ethnic motivations that arise within the local context. The way in which the
Taliban—which is essentially to say Mullah Omar—was willing to sacrifice governmental power for the sake of international solidarity was an entirely exceptional event, but it was
precisely what brought about the regime's collapse. The American bombing revealed a popular discontent with the Taliban
which Mullah Omar's strategy had not taken into account. The
reasons for the decline and fall of the Taliban were tribal—and,
paradoxically, nationalist. The treatment of prisoners and the
evident half-heartedness of the fighting between Afghans, as distinct from that between the Afghans of the Northern Alliance
and the Islamic volunteers, demonstrate that even after twenty
years of war and ethnic polarisation, the sense of Afghan national identity had remained strong. In fact, the intensely ideo-

logical nature of both the language and the practices of the Taliban served, because of their excesses, to alienate the people and thus exclude for the foreseeable future a role for radical Islam. Fundamentalism in its cultural and social forms will no doubt persist, especially in the tribal regions, but a long time will certainly elapse before it again takes political form. In a sense it was transnational Islamism carried to the extreme which destroyed both the Taliban regime and Afghan internationalism. The limit of the global movements has been reached: they come up against a barrier when local priorities begin once again to reassert themselves.

Other more material factors were also in play, but discreetly, since they were diametrically opposed to the values publicly espoused by the radical movements. These were ethnic, tribal and social considerations. Here again the triumph of the local over the global showed itself. The ethnic dimension, which in Central Asia adopts a nationalistic form, was particularly strong among the Pushtuns. Pushtun domination of the Islamic movements was to be seen among Qazi Hussein's Jamaat-i-Islami and the Jami'at-i-Ulema-i-Islam of Maulana Sami ul-Haq and Maulana Fazlur Rehman. However the dialectic between Pushtun identity and that of Islamic neo-fundamentalism operated in two directions. It gave a boost to fundamentalist Pushtun movements like the Taliban which, some time after the capture of Kabul by Massoud in 1992, reasserted Pushtun supremacy. Even royalists such as Hamid Karzai, at least for a period of some months, adhered at a particular moment to the Taliban, as did former Communists such as the Afghan General Tana'y. However, the tendency was reversible. In November 2001 tribal combatants of former Taliban allegiance rallied to Hamid Karzai. Finally, ethnic factors also served to set limits to the Taliban—which northern Afghanistan resisted not because it was more secularised but because it perceived the Taliban as an incarnation of Pushtun hegemonism.

At a less elevated level it was feasible for a fundamentalist movement to come into existence based on purely tribal

considerations. This was the case with the TNSM led by Sufi
Muhammad in the Malakand region, the emirates of Nuristan
and the Pesh valley. Tribal issues were deeply embedded in
the neo-fundamentalist movements, as became evident at the
fall of Kandahar in December 2001 when the Taliban negoti-
ated with a group of tribal chiefs each of whom was attempting to protect his own people. The dialectic between Islamism
and tribalism was complex. The Taliban were both the protagonists of the phenomena of detribalisation, and its outcome,
as was illustrated both in the crisis of the traditional élites and
by the attacks mounted against customary law in the name of
the Shari'a.

The radical movements were therefore constantly under
pressure from above—by means of internationalist influences
which spoke the same language—and from below by local imperatives, which were often in practice disregarded but which
continued nevertheless to conflict with the movements' formal
ideology. This double reference made such movements vulnerable at times of serious crisis, since the resurgence of local
motivations weakened them.

The question which therefore arises is: to what extent can
real internationalism be identified? Although this study has
identified certain focal points in Pakistan such as al-Qaida, the
coordination of the Pakistani religious movements, and the ISI,
the relationship between these three is more arbitrary than
structural. In fact Bin Laden's operative networks are more in
Europe than in Pakistan. Volunteers are sent by European mosques, and the names of those involved in the process recur frequently. The list includes Abu Hamza, an Egyptian; Sheikh
Bakri, a Syrian; Yasir al-Sirri, an Egyptian who is said to have
provided credentials for Masood's assassins; Abu Qatada, (real
name Omar Abu Omar), a Palestinian travelling on a Jordanian
passport who is said also to be a member of Al-Muhajirun and
of the *fatwa* committee of al-Qaida;[6] and Abderraouf Hannashi,

---

[6] According to a renegade, Al Fadl, see the *New York Times*, 21 February 2001.

imam of a mosque in Montreal, who harboured Ahmed Ressam.[7] The persons specified have all denied being members of al-Qaida, even though Bakri has openly supported it and Abu Qatada is said to have been a member of the al-Qaida council for fatwas.[8] In fact these imams address an audience composed of second-generation Muslims of very varied ethnic and national origins. It is evident that the West is an important element in the construction of the networks which operate in Afghanistan.

True internationalism therefore relates to circles which are already globalised, which are in search of roots or new identities, and which mobilise around the issues of *jihad* and the *umma*. However, the defeat suffered in 2001 with the fall of Kabul illustrates the limits of a mobilisation unable to reach beyond radical circles. The sole exception is where it links itself to local motivations: this is therefore both its strength and its weakness.

---

[7] Josh Meyer, "Terrorist says plans didn't end …", *Los Angeles Times*, 4 July 2001.
[8] There is often strong criticism of Bakri even in Islamist circles, accusing him of revealing the names of combatants who have gone to Afghanistan.

6. Conclusion

It was in the 1990s that Islamism became more and more anti-Western—or, more accurately, anti-American. The language of the *jihad* tended initially to relate to the promotion of the Shari'a and the construction of an Islamic society. The Taliban emerged in 1994 as a conservative Sunni movement close to the Saudi Wahhabis but also to the Americans. It also drew closer to Osama Bin Laden's al-Qaida organisation, and was thus typical of the process of radicalisation and especially of the internationalisation of certain movements. Another instance was the Islamic Movement of Uzbekistan (IMU). This operated at first entirely within the Uzbek community, but after 1998 threw in its lot wholly with the Taliban and al-Qaida—to the extent that its principal leader Juma Namangani and hundreds of his men were killed during the American bombing of northern Afghanistan in November 2001. The terrorist attacks of 11 September were therefore at one and the same time a consequence and a cause of the radicalisation and the internationalisation of the Islamist movements of the region. In fact it is the extent of the armed and militant involvement of any one of the various movements in the battle against the American intervention—or, on the other hand, of their passivity—that enables it to be classified as either radical or moderate.

Today, therefore, it is the degree of anti-Americanism which allows the radicalism of a movement to be measured, rather than its commitment to promotion of the Shari'a. The line is drawn very clearly in Afghanistan, with the Taliban and al-Qaida against all the others, although in Central Asia and Pakistan it is more blurred. In Central Asia the IMU was found alongside the Taliban, while the Tajik PRI joined the anti-terrorist coalition. The Hizb ul-Tahrir, newly arrived as a member of the Islamic agglomeration, shared many ideas with al-Qaida, such as the primacy of the *umma* over the nation-state, the construction of the Caliphate as a bulwark against Western hegemony, the rejection of dialogue with Western civilisation, and the view of Christianity and Judaism as institutionally inimical to Islam. On the other hand, none of its members joined the armed struggle either in Central Asia or in Afghanistan, and it was not listed by the Pentagon as a terrorist organisation. No doubt believing that the armed struggle had been launched prematurely, Hizb ul-Tahrir held aloof.

In Pakistan the radical religious tendency united to coordinate support for the Taliban under the banner of the Pakistan-Afghanistan Committee, which included thirty-seven organisations. However, after adopting a very hard line and encouraging volunteers to join the fight in Afghanistan, this body suddenly moderated its tone, partly as the result of pressure brought to bear by General Musharraf and partly because of the shock of the fall of Kabul on 13 November 2001.

The defeat of the Taliban regime in Afghanistan therefore had substantial consequences for the region. These included the delinkage of Central Asia from the Pakistani radical tendency and the probable disappearance of the Islamic radical movements in Afghanistan, leading to the return of ethnic and tribal motivations and the "warlord" system, which may in future be supplanted in their turn by the restoration of national identity.

The Afghan campaign was marked by a severe defeat for the jihadists, who had imagined that the West, with its intrinsic weaknesses, would be unable to campaign in Afghanistan, or would become bogged down at a moment when a wave of sympathy for the new *mujahidin* fighting in Afghanistan would rally the masses in the Muslim world. Bin Laden's calendar was based on this plan. Anticipating the American reaction to the attack on the World Trade Centre, although he could not have been aware of the precise date and time when this would occur, he strove to strengthen his hold on the territory of Afghanistan in order to deprive the Americans of any possible bridgehead. The assassination of General Massoud on 9 September 2001 was dictated by the same logic. However, the plan failed because Massoud was killed too late, or because the attack on the World Trade Centre occurred too soon. In short, when the Americans attacked on 7 October 2001 they benefited from a decisive bridgehead in the shape of the Northern Alliance.

Whatever the context, the jihadists lost all the more decisively because of the rapid and easy American victory. Afghan support for the Americans was effective and conspicuous, they suffered few losses, the Afghan Taliban fighters were routed, and the foreign volunteers were crushed in spite of their fierce resistance. There was little significant reaction in the Arab world, and only the feeblest of demonstrations were mounted in Pakistan.

However this jihadist defeat did not necessarily signify a decline of "ummist" militancy, preaching the restoration of the *umma*. On the contrary it tended to benefit the preaching faction, which thought that any recourse to arms was premature before the social basis of the Muslim communities had been re-mobilised and transformed along Islamic lines. In the whole region it was Hizb ul-Tahrir which would profit directly from the crisis. Those who prioritise the *da'wa* ahead of the *jihad* were able to assert that Bin Laden had put the cart before the horse by launching a *jihad* against the United States before the Muslim community was ready to carry out a war in which it proved to be more a spectator than an actor. The radical tendency in Central Asia will no doubt reconstruct itself, probably around Hizb ul-Tahrir which has always regarded any uprising as premature.

The fact that the *Salafi* community will probably become a preaching rather than a jihadist institution does not mean that appeals to conflict will in future be suppressed; rather, it means that they will be concerned with precise areas, where jihadism and a national liberation movement go hand in hand, such as Palestine, Kashmir and Chechnya. The defeat of the Taliban and Bin Laden will not signify any lessening of the intensity of struggles undertaken in a national and Muslim framework; it is more probable that there will be a diminution of armed and transnational militant Islamism in favour of a more deep-rooted movement of preaching (*da'awa*) and re-Islamisation.

In so far as it concerns the region under discussion here, Central Asia is likely to see the appeal of *jihad* diminish in favour of a more clandestine and less political kind of activism. Residual Taliban resistance is not very likely, except in the tribal area close to the Pakistan border, where it would be backed by the radical elements who, in the wake of the MMA's electoral victory, will benefit from the creation of some sort of 'Talibanisation' in the NWFP and part of Baluchistan. More probable is a move back towards tribal imperatives, in the context of a re-structuring of the balance of power between the ethnic groups. However a neo-fundamentalism appropriate to tribal circles—which are close to the social ideas of the Taliban—can be expected to continue dominating life in many tribal areas, while staying at a personal, non-political level.

In Pakistan jihadist language will be directed more towards Kashmir. The radical religious parties have retained their structures and remain intact. There has been neither an American intervention nor a wave of mass arrests. The radical leaders were merely under house arrest, and restrictions on their movements have been relaxed. Almost all of the militants detained in 2002 have been released as the courts could not find sufficient evidence to continue holding them. No effort has been made to disarm the groups, several of them have reconstituted under different names and are again raising money, albeit a little more discreetly, and proselytising for *jihad*. The Harakat ul Muja-hidin (alias Harakat ul Ansar alias Jamiat ul Ansar) and the Harakat al Jihad al Islami (HUJI) have not been banned, most probably because of their large following in the lower and middle ranks of the Pakistan army. Fazlul Rehman Khalil, leader of the HUM and one of the first signatories of the fatwa issued in 1998 by Osama Bin Laden against the United States and Israel, as well as Qari Saifullah Akhtar, leader of the HUJI, were not arrested. Moreover, the ban of 12 January 2002 did not cover Azad Kashmir, the Northern Areas and the tribal areas (FATA), which enabled the movements to transfer their infrastructure and their cadres to these regions where they were asked to keep a low profile for some time. The radicals are forcefully revising their positions on the Kashmir issue, which is the only location in which *jihad* continues to make sense, since the Americans, who do not want to destabilise General Musharraf, have not applied the same rigour to the groups operating in Kashmir as has faced those who fought in Afghanistan. Kashmir has taken the place of Afghanistan as an emblem of *jihad*.

The trial of strength in Afghanistan has in the first place militated in favour of General Musharraf, who is assured of American support, has retained the Islamic bomb, and has easily confronted popular demonstrations which were less than massive. Although public opinion in Pakistan is highly critical of the American intervention, it is also critical of the religious radicals. Although General Musharraf faces a serious risk of assassination,[1] but the Americans regard him as a stabilising factor. Nevertheless, Pakistan provides shelter for thousands of Afghan former Taliban, Arab volunteers and Pakistani veterans of the Afghan *jihad*. The government makes efforts to expel foreigners: over 450, about 200 of them Yemenis and Saudis, have been captured in Pakistan in 125 raids and handed over to the American authorities, they constitute two thirds of the Guantanamo detainees but it can hardly act against Pakistani citizens or against Afghan Pushtuns, who can easily obtain

---

[1] Two plots were foiled in April and in September 2002. A Rangers (paramiliary force) inspector, Wasim Akhtar, was arrested for his involvement in the first plot.

Pakistani identity papers. The Pushtun regions, where there are military training camps, are poised to become a new base for radical Islamic agitation. This has become a fact since the elections of 10 October 2002 which enabled the Islamic parties constituting the Muttahida Majlis-e Amal to come to power in the North West Frontier Province (NWFP) and to be part of a coalition government in Baluchistan. This was followed by an upsurge of attacks against the American troops in the Pushtun provinces of Afghanistan bordering Pakistan—where the attackers can find a safe haven and where Al Qaida militants are said to be running training camps—and by unprecedented sectarian attacks against Shiites in Quetta from May 2003. Under American pressure, Pakistan sent troops—sometimes accompanied by American Special Forces teams—into the tribal areas for the first time since 1947, which created unrest and further radicalised the local Pushtuns. However, the religious radicals' room for manoeuvre is reduced. Above all, the Pakistani government will unquestionably find itself obliged to revise its policy of tolerance towards the Islamist movements.

The crisis in jihadist and internationalist ideology has resulted in the absence of real international solidarity and, with the return to Afghanistan of the traditional rationales of political alignments, opportunistic alliances and parallel relations between tribes and ethnic groups at the expense of international solidarity. In this respect the great lesson of the American campaign of 2001 related to the linkage between the hyperpower and local forces, to the detriment of transnational networks. After the United States had ignored the Northern Alliance for ten years, the sudden cooperation between them—allying the B52 bomber with the fighter on horseback—illustrated how the followers of the late General Massoud were able to profit from their sudden arrival centre-stage, while continuing to pursue their own aims.

Thus the military campaign of October and November 2001 considerably weakened the transnational Islamic networks and reinforced state and nationalist influences in the entire region under examination, though without wholly effacing the Islamic aspect of mobilisation, which seems destined to take a more socio-cultural form than a directly political one. The fate of the last jihadists is being played out in Pakistan. They have decided to engage in confrontation with President Musharraf's regime, which will have no option but to suppress them—at the price of undermining its own position in the conflict with India over Kashmir.

Before 11 September the objectives of the jihadist movement in Pakistan were different from those of the jihadist movements in Arab countries, and from those of Bin Laden. They were more in line with the regional strategy of the Pakistan government, and the interest of the radicals, as beneficiaries of the existing social and political order, was in maintaining the *status quo*. The state and the Islamist movements had common interests, which was not the case in the Arab countries. Although at the outset the social base of these movements was restricted, the state took them to itself and agreed with them a type of partnership both to pursue external political objectives and to control the major centrist parties—principally the Pakistan People's Party and the Muslim League—which had at their disposal a broad and reliable constituency. Islamism was directed not against the state but against local sectarian targets such as the Shi'ites, the Christians and the Ahmadis, or externally against infidels such as the Hindus. A substantial number of these movements, if not all of them, served as instruments of Pakistan's regional policy and constituted both an advance-guard and a reserve. The army needed of them as much as they needed the army.

However, 11 September changed the pattern. Within a few hours General Musharraf accepted the American conditions. He abandoned the Taliban, but at the same time he attempted to avoid a direct confrontation with the Pakistani radicals, appeasing them by relaunching the Kashmir conflict and threatening to use his nuclear weapons in the event of an Indian attack. Before 11 September Musharraf's position had been to ally himself secretly with the jihadists, while in public keeping his distance from the religious parties and promoting a moderate image of himself in order to win Western approval and gain economic support. After 11 September, and particularly after the 13 December attack on the Indian Parliament, he played a double game by giving the impression that he was yielding to American and Indian pressure, while at the same time he offered reassurance to the jihadists. He achieved this by making repeated declarations on the Kashmiri issue, freeing arrested militants, not implementing repressive measures in Azad Kashmir to which the militants had retreated, and taking no action over the *madrasas* despite of Western pressure for their reform. Meanwhile he requested the militants to keep a low profile, and gave them his word that he would not prejudice their ability to wage *jihad* against India. However, this ambiguous policy was destined to fail, and gradually, under the constraint of American and Indian pressures and stirrings among radicals, Musharraf was obliged to move towards the option he had not wished for, namely to align himself completely with the Americans and to crack down on the radicals.

General Musharraf's address to the nation on 12 January 2002 was the moment when a real break occurred—not only with the era of General Zia ul-Haq but also with his own earlier declarations, particularly concerning Kashmir and Afghanistan. He underlined the primacy of the state and the nation over all forms of pan-Islamism and, by setting aside General Zia ul-Haq's policy of Islamisation, emphasised once more the bond between Pakistan's historical destiny and the project conceived by the country's founder Muhammad Ali Jinnah. This was a debate to which Pakistan had often returned since 1947. The issue was whether the country, created as a state for the Muslims of the Indian sub-continent, should be primarily an Islamic state, with the vocation of representing and defending all those who fought in their capacity as Muslims. This had been the vision of Maulana Maududi, General Zia ul-Haq, and the religious radicals. Or was Pakistan just one nation-state among others, for which national interests should come before Islamic solidarity? In fact, from General Zia ul-Haq's take-over of power in 1977 the Islamist movements, both Pakistani and Afghan, had been made use of by the state, but the state in exchange afforded them a wide field of action, and in the end they had imposed their agenda in both internal and external affairs.

Musharraf's address to the nation marked a clear break with this policy in both at home and abroad. His main points were as follows. He argued, first, that the state should exercise a mo-nopoly over external policy to be determined not by Islamic solidarity but by the country's national interests. Pakistan was a territorial nation-state, not an ideological state. He employed the expressions "nation", "soil" and "territory" while never stressing the word "*jihad*", even in connection with Kashmir, and Afghanistan was spoken of for the first time as a foreign country. He expressed no preference as between the factions, and described the Northern Alliance, opposed to the Taliban, as Muslim. Pakistan would neither make any demand nor in-dulge in any recrimination over the ethnic balance in Afghani-stan—a change from Musharraf's previous statements, in which he had said explicitly that "it is in Pakistan's interests to have a Pushtun regime in Kabul", and from those of his foreign min-ister, who had said "Northern Alliance domination is unac-ceptable for Pakistan."

Musharraf went on to say that Kashmir was a bilateral prob-lem which should be resolved between India and Pakistan, with the Kashmiris also having their say, while United Nations resolutions were respected. Kashmir, he asserted, was not an Is-lamic issue, while the radical movements based in Pakistan—which, it should be recalled, he had himself made use of during the Kargil conflict in 1999—were to be kept out of play, pref-erence being given to the authentically Kashmiri movements which had been marginalised by Islamabad since the 1990s. This was an invitation to bilateral negotiation between India and the Kashmiris, which had up till then been rejected by

New Delhi, but which would enable a resolution of the conflict saving the face of both countries by granting greater autonomy within the Union of India. Implicitly Musharraf renounced all claims to Kashmir, while in the interior context he advocated a depoliticisation of Islam for the benefit of the state. To this end the state should embark on the suppression of radical groups and control the networks of *madrasas*. This was to be achieved by imposing a more modern curriculum, standardising qualifications, registering schools before they could be allowed to operate, imposing checks on foreign students, and finally by a process of state licensing of imams authorised to preach sermons, while others were restricted to leading prayers. Islam was to become a national phenomenon, though without being a function of the state. Complete "laicisation" was not in question. Pakistan continued to affirm its status as a Muslim state, on the model of Egypt or Morocco.

Confrontation between Musharraf and the radicals therefore seemed inevitable, especially since the Americans kept up their pressure. Following 11 September, and especially following his speech on 12 January, the radicals felt themselves betrayed and abandoned. From this point on their principal objective was to destabilise Musharraf, killing him if necessary, and to provoke a war between India and Pakistan. While the "Great Jihad" was in abeyance they would pursue their local *jihad*. The more the Musharraf government seemed to be weakened and under the domination of the United States, the more active did the jihadist movements become. This accounts for the re-emergence of violence after the referendum of 30 April 2002, which confirmed Musharraf in his position for a further five years but destroyed his credibility.

At the time of writing, it is clear that armed conflict carried on by the jihadists is the affair of Pakistan alone. However, it retains a strong international dimension there because of the presence in the country of so many Arab volunteers and Afghan partisans. This international dimension has been strengthened by the tension between India and Pakistan in Kashmir, which has obliged the United States to be active in the region. The Pakistani military establishment's attitude towards *jidahi* organisations involved in Kashmir is very ambiguous. The groups have apparently been told to remove the United States from their agenda and to focus on Kashmir. In the absence of a breakthrough in Kashmir, the army will need the *jihadis* to put pressure on India, and if the peace initiative launched in May 2003 does not succeed, there will be an upsurge of infiltrations in Kashmir. Finally, the continued presence of US troops in Afghanistan can only offer a target to the radicals who have retreated to Pakistan. Today more than ever, therefore, Pakistan continues to be the central point of the mobilisation of the Islamic radicals.

Select Bibliography

J. Burke, *al-Qaeda: Casting a Shadow of Terror*, London: I. B. Tauris, 2003.

G. Dorronsoro, *La révolution afghane. Des communistes aux taliban*, Paris: Karthala, 2000; transl. as *Afghanistan: Revolution Unending, 1979–2002*, London: Hurst, 2004.

Y. Fouda and N. Fielding, *Masterminds of terror*, Edinburgh: Mainstream, 2003.

S. Ganguly, *The Crisis in Kashmir: Portents of War, Hopes of Peace*, New York: Cambridge University Press, 1999.

M. Griffin, *Reaping the Whirlwind: the Taliban Movement in Afghanistan*, London: Pluto Press, 2001.

R. Gunaratna, *Inside Al Qaeda: Global Network of Terror*, London: Hurst, 2002.

V. Hewitt, *Reclaiming the Past: the Search for Political and Cultural Unity in Contemporary Jammu and Kashmir*, London: Portland, 1995.

Ch. Jaffrelot (ed.), *Le Pakistan, carrefour de tensions régionales*, Bruxelles: Éditions Complexe, 2002.

——— (ed.), *A History of Pakistan and its Origins*, London: Anthem Press, 2002.

——— (ed.), *Pakistan: Nationalism without a Nation?*, London: Zed Books, 2002.

W. Maley (ed.). *Fundamentalism reborn? Afghanistan and the Taliban*, London: Hurst, 1998.

S.V.R. Nasr, *The Vanguard of the Islamic Revolution: The Jama'at-i islami of Pakistan*, Berkeley: University of California Press, 1994.

B. Puri, *Kashmir: Towards Insurgency*, London: Sangam Books, 1993.

J.-L. Racine, *Cachemire. Au péril de la guerre*, Paris: Autrement, 2002.

A. Rashid, *Taliban: Islam, Oil and the New Great Game in Central Asia*, London: I. B. Tauris, 2000.

———, *Jihad: the Rise of Militant Islam in Central Asia*, New Haven: Yale University Press, 2002, New York University Press, 2000.

O. Roy, *La nouvelle Asie centrale ou la fabrication des nations*, Paris: Seuil, 1997.

———, *Globalised Islam: Fundamentalism, De-territorialisation and the Search for the New 'Ummah*, London: Hurst, 2004.

I. Talbot, *Pakistan: a Modern History*, London: Hurst, 1999.

Index